l3

The Divided House

The Divided House

Women at Westminster

Melanie Phillips

SIDGWICK & JACKSON

LONDON

First published in Great Britain in 1980
by Sidgwick and Jackson Limited

Copyright © 1980 by Melanie Phillips

ISBN 0 283 98547 X

Phototypeset in Monophoto Garamond by
Servis Filmsetting Limited, Manchester
Printed in Great Britain by
Biddles Limited, Martyr Road, Guildford
for Sidgwick and Jackson Limited
1 Tavistock Chambers, Bloomsbury Way
London WC1A 2SG

For Joshua

Acknowledgements

Many people provided invaluable help with this book. During my research, I interviewed more than forty women politicians. They generously made time to see me, even though many of them were badgered by constant requests from all over the world for information about themselves. I am also indebted to their colleagues who asked to remain anonymous but who furnished many valuable insights.

I am particularly grateful to the staff of the splendid Fawcett library, who provided enthusiastic guidance through their collection of specialist books and documents. I appreciated the help provided at Transport House, particularly by Joyce Gould, the Chief Women's Officer of the Labour Party, and by the staff of the Labour Party library. I am also grateful to Angela Hooper, the Chief Woman Executive of the Conservative Party, and to the press department at Conservative Central Office. My thanks to the staff of the Equal Opportunities Commission, to Edna Healey for her encouragement and to Joy Melville for her guidance. I am indebted, finally, to Sue Summers, whose idea started this project, and above all to Joshua Rozenberg, whose painstaking support ensured that it was finished.

Contents

CONTENTS

List of Illustrations

Introduction

ANY study of women Members of Parliament will invariably provoke some raised eyebrows. Why should women in particular be the subject of scrutiny? After all, a woman is now Prime Minister; sex discrimination is illegal; and it is high time that women were treated on their merits as individuals rather than as a group whose every step into public life is viewed as a symbolic action worthy of note. None of these points can be denied. But equally irrefutable is the fact that at the General Election in 1979, only nineteen women were returned to Westminster among 635 M.P.s. In more than half a century of theoretical equality in political life, the number of women M.P.s has remained derisory – which makes Margaret Thatcher's achievement in becoming Prime Minister thoroughly remarkable.

Their very rarity marks out these women M.P.s as special people, interesting because they have managed to penetrate an institution which largely remains a gentlemen's club. So what kind of people are they? This book is not an academic exercise; it is not a comprehensive history of the achievements of women at Westminster, nor is it a sociological analysis. Instead, it looks at the qualities that brought these women to Parliament, at their backgrounds and upbringing, at their reasons for wanting to become politicians, at the difficulties they overcame to be selected as candidates, at the pressures they have faced in reconciling their public and private lives, and at the way they are perceived by the press and public.

I have confined myself to women at Westminster, rather than across the spectrum of political life, for two reasons. The national forum of Parliamentary politics seems to me to throw into vivid relief the problems women have to overcome in public life and the characteristics they require to succeed. Moreover, if the inquiry were extended to women in trade unions and local government, logic would dictate its further extension to Whitehall and from there to other comparable professions; the study of women in politics would become a study of women in society. So the book is based largely on interviews I have conducted with women who are current or former M.P.s and with women who have entered national politics through the back door of the House of Lords.

Three women, Mrs Barbara Castle, Mrs Shirley Williams and Mrs Margaret Thatcher, are paid special attention as the three most renowned and able women in post-war Parliamentary politics. Of these three, only Mrs Thatcher felt unable to grant me an interview. However, with the aid of colleagues who had worked closely with her, and with the help of others who had worked with Mrs Castle and Mrs Williams, as well as by drawing upon the archives of material documenting their lives, I have been able to draw comparisons between their characters, public images and careers. I have tried to set their achievements, and those of all the other women in Parliament, in some context by including a brief history of the fight by women to achieve equality in national politics. I have also looked closely at women who are now life peers although they were never elected to Parliament; if these women are political animals, did they avoid the House of Commons by mischance or design? There is a chapter devoted to the treatment of women in politics by the press; and the book concludes with an analysis of attitudes and an attempt to resolve the thorny question of whether women politicians should act as a cohesive group or merge as individuals into the grand Parliamentary design.

Melanie Phillips
November 1979

1 *The Making of a Prime Minister*

WHEN Margaret Thatcher was elected leader of the Conservative Party in 1975, there was almost as much delight among the ranks of the then Labour Cabinet as there was among her own supporters. Lady Falkender, who as Marcia Williams was then Harold Wilson's political secretary, remembers the scene well. 'When the election happened, the Cabinet had been meeting at the Commons, so they all hung around waiting for the result to be announced – and when it was they all burst out in great glee, saying, "We're home and dry!" But only a couple of the more perceptive ones, including Peter Shore, realised that as a woman she would have a number of advantages that none of us would talk about. The women in the country would identify with her; and if you could then project forward to visualise a government which was going to be unpopular and produce a swing in the masculine vote based on a desire for change, then you could see the danger. But only a couple of them did so.'

The Cabinet's reaction was understandable. The Conservatives had, apparently, hung an albatross around their necks in their overwhelming desire to rid themselves of an unpopular leader who was an electoral liability. They had replaced a stiff-necked man who lacked the common touch with a woman whose cultivated accent and appearance were almost a caricature of the twinset-and-pearls party faithful, themselves a stereotype in the popular imagination. Ordinary people, it seemed, could not possibly identify with her; she represented extreme right-wing policies – the unacceptably vicious face of Conservatism – which would alienate the crucial political centre ground courted by Edward Heath; the only experience she had had of Government was as Education Secretary, for which she was remembered mainly as the 'milk-snatcher'; and to cap it all she was a woman. And everyone knew, after all, that even women did not really approve of women politicians, let alone a woman Prime Minister.

The disastrous error of such thinking was finally revealed on 4 May, 1979, when Mrs Thatcher won the general election with a substantial overall majority, quite enough to keep her in power until 1984. The curious thing was that the assessment of her characteristics and unpopularity had not been proved wrong. James Callaghan, the defeated Prime Minister, was constantly shown by opinion polls to be streets ahead of Mrs Thatcher in personal popularity – the same opinion polls that foretold the fate of his government. Labour Party canvassers were cheered, and Conservatives dismayed, by the unmistakeable unpopularity of Mrs Thatcher that was displayed on countless doorsteps. So why were the Tories elected? It is a truism that Oppositions do not win general elections, Governments lose them. But whatever the reasons for that election result – lack of really socialist policies, fear of more socialist policies, the unpopularity of the unions following the winter of strikes – it is clear that the deep desire for change in the country produced an unstoppable momentum which swept the Conservatives to power with Mrs Thatcher at their helm – and people simply shut their eyes to the unattractive aspects of her personality.

A similar process had operated to enable her to topple Edward Heath in the leadership struggle. It is important to understand that episode in order to begin to understand Mrs Thatcher's character and why it was that she became Britain's first woman Prime Minister. If anyone had been asked in 1974, before the fall of Mr Heath, whether Mrs Thatcher was more suitable for the job than Shirley Williams or Barbara Castle, the answer would surely have been ribaldly negative. She had not had, after all, a particularly notable Parliamentary career. Apart from her time as Education Secretary, her only claim to renown was a handful of good speeches in the Commons – where the standard of her performances was patchy – and the high esteem of a few people who had watched her closely. The suggestion that she might lead the party was being mooted in 1974, but half-incredulously. The *Daily Express* of 9 April of that year caught the mood: 'Do you fall off your chair laughing at the idea of Mrs

NANCY ASTOR campaigning in Plymouth in 1919 (above), the election that took her into Parliament, and in the 1920s

"THE ANGEL IN 'THE HOUSE;'" OR, THE RESULT OF FEMALE SUFFRAGE.
(*A Troubled Dream of the Future.*)

PUNCH EATS HIS WORDS
The first cartoon appeared on
14 June 1884, the second on
10 December 1919

THE PENITENT.

MR. PUNCH, ALWAYS READY TO ADMIT HIS EXCEPTIONAL "BLOOMERS," DO
PENANCE FOR HIS ERROR OF THIRTY-FIVE YEARS AGO, AND BEGS TO OFFER HI
RESPECTFUL CONGRATULATIONS TO LADY ASTOR, M.P.

MARGARET WINTRINGHAM, elected to her husband's
constituency, Louth, in 1921 after his death. As a mark of respect to
her husband she did not speak in public throughout the campaign

SUSAN LAWRENCE, one of the first three Labour candidates to
be elected in 1923. She was a Conservative supporter until she learnt
how poorly paid the London County Council charwomen were; she
then promptly resigned her Council seat and joined the Labour Party

ELLEN WILKINSON, known as 'Red Ellen' or 'The Fiery Particle',
speaking at a peace demonstration in September 1938. She was elected Labour
M.P. for Jarrow in 1924

The Rt Hon. MARGARET BONDFIELD, as Minister of Labour the
first woman Cabinet Minister. She is pictured here in 1929 with J.J. Lawson,
Parliamentary Secretary to the Ministry of Labour

Thatcher becoming Tory leader? There are hard, shrewd men in the Tory Party, I can tell you, who do not.' Barbara Castle was by then too old to be considered in the running for the Labour leadership when it fell vacant, but in the past many have seen in her the qualities that could have taken her to the top. And Shirley Williams, although now out of Parliament altogether, is still talked of as a possible contender for the leadership, heir as she is of Gaitskell and Crosland and a leader of the party's right wing. But those who know these women well say that neither of them, if confronted with similar circumstances to those which faced Margaret Thatcher when she made her bid for the leadership, would have seized the opportunity as she did.

The reason for Mrs Thatcher's success was a combination of courage and brutal determination; these were the key factors that enabled her to make the most of an opportunity that had luckily presented itself to her. Almost until the last moment she discounted any thought that she might be elected leader of the party, maintaining that neither the party nor the country was ready for a woman leader. The *Financial Times* on 31 September 1974 quoted her as saying that the election of a party leader 'is an emotional business, involving a person being in the right place at the right time. It will be years – and not in my time – that a woman will lead the party or become Prime Minister.' On 23 September the *Evening News* reported her as saying: 'I don't want to be leader of the party. I'm happy to be in the top dozen. Being leader means total commitment. But I have a family.' But the prize for carrying her most disingenuous comment of all at this time must be awarded to the *Daily Mail*, which was amused to note that she was apparently bored by all these suggestions that she or Shirley Williams might become Prime Minister, since it had never before crossed her mind.

A few months later, however, after Sir Keith Joseph had decided not to stand for the leadership, Mrs Thatcher decided to go for bust. 'I heard that Keith Joseph was not going to run against Ted. Someone had to. I said to Keith, "If you are not, I shall." There was no hesitation, there was no doubt, there has been no doubt since. It might have put me on the back benches for life, or out, I did not know. But the one thing I seemed to have was the power to make a decision when a decision had to be made.' It was a unique set of circumstances: the backbenchers' desire to be rid of Edward Heath, the fact that no one else of any substance was prepared to stand against him, the exceptional skill of Mrs Thatcher's campaign manager, and her own gambler's courage. One of her colleagues remarked to me: 'There was this inexplicable gut reaction among the backbenchers. I would say to them, but she's a woman; they would say, yes, but . . . What they were wanting was a new leader and Margaret stood for something definitely different. And her campaign was very skilful.' Typically, Mrs Thatcher herself did not acknowledge the powerful coincidences that gave her victory. When asked why she thought she had won, she replied crisply in one word: 'Merit.' She had reacted in a similar fashion when she won a poetry-reading prize as a child. The nine-year-old's prize may have been translated into a greater reward, but the sentiment hadn't changed.

Until that period, Mrs Thatcher's greatest ambition had been to become Chancellor of the Exchequer – although, again, she didn't think the party would allow a woman to occupy the post. When the opportunity arose to try to snatch the biggest prize of all, she knew full well that she was taking an enormous risk in terms of her own career but it was a risk that she chose to take. Barbara Castle, say her friends, would not have done the same. She is as tough as Mrs Thatcher, and if she had become Prime Minister would have brought to the job as much steely determination, but she would not have been capable of being as ruthless on her own behalf. For although she is also a courageous woman, her mind would have dwelt on the possibility of failure, and the thought of failing and being cast into the wilderness as a result would have held her back. Similarly, Shirley Williams would also probably have failed to seize the moment. Apart from her own doubts about making that level of commitment to political life, she is said to lack the element of ruthlessness necessary for such manoeuvres. Determined and principled as she is, she is not at ease amidst intrigue and political manoeuvring. This uncertainty showed itself, for example, in the confused vote she cast for an anti-market ploy on the Party's National Executive Committee, although she herself is so passionately pro-European that she threatened to leave politics if Labour took Britain out of Europe.

Barbara Castle was always extremely concerned about her own courage, always afraid that she would let herself down, fail by her own standards. In 1966, two years before the great battle over *In Place of Strife*, her proposals for changes in industrial relations which almost destroyed her politically, she told David Mason of the *Irish Press*: 'I despise myself for moments of political cowardice or calculation. I've this great fear of cowardice – like finding oneself in a cinema and stampeding for the exit if a fire broke out. I suppose I'm less tense than I used to be, but when I first got up to speak my hands used to tremble so much I could hardly hold the paper. The beastlier people are to me, the more sure I am of my rightness. To go down fighting with no thought of humiliation or abdication, that's life's biggest thrill.'

Hers is the sort of courage that displays itself when she is under threat, that responds to events once they have happened. As she remarked when asked if she wanted to be Prime Minister: 'If the challenge came I would enjoy it. I never have sought out any of the jobs that have come to me; they just sort of happen. I think that, you know, if it had been a question of sitting down and planning for or working for something or aspiring to something my courage would have run out. I go through life cheekily, if you like, putting myself into situations and then I think, my goodness! Make or break, this one . . . better have a quick shot at this, I really have stuck my neck out here.'

Nevertheless, there have been few Cabinet Ministers who have bettered her record of fighting in Cabinet, particularly against the Treasury, to get the policies she wanted through and to get more money for her department of state. Mrs Thatcher had a similar reputation when she was Secretary of State for Education. 'You've got to hand it to her,' said one educationalist who would not count himself among her supporters, 'if she was convinced of something, she wasn't afraid to tackle her senior colleagues in Cabinet. In the 1972 pay dispute, she went back to the Cabinet committee *twice* to fight the case for the teachers; she wasn't cowed.' Both she and Mrs Castle are also superb political operators, especially when it comes to getting themselves out of trouble. Mrs Thatcher once remarked admiringly of Barbara Castle that whatever she did wrong, and whatever the Labour government did wrong, the mud miraculously never stuck on Barbara. But she achieved precisely the same sleight of hand when she wrested the leadership from Edward Heath, the Prime Minister in whose government she had served and with whose policies she had been identified as a senior Minister – the very policies she then denounced, with no shred of blame attaching to herself for having helped put them into practice.

People never like to think of themselves as ruthless individuals, and women politicians may tend to over-emphasise their concern about human problems to counter such an impression, not least in their own minds. Mrs Thatcher, it seems, is no exception. On 23 September 1974, she chortled to John Evans of the London *Evening News*: 'I really am astonished at the impression people have of me. It's now being said that

I'm ruthlessly ambitious. In fact, I'm not ruthless. I just stick to my guns. But people don't understand. I'm just an ordinary working wife. I trot up to the launderette.' Tales about her generosity towards individuals and concern over their personal problems abound. People relate how she will ask them sympathetically about personal domestic crises of which they had no idea she was aware. Yet at the same time even her friends find in her a paradoxical iciness from which they recoil. One such friend said she found this hard to explain: 'I've known her for a long time, and consider myself her friend, but there's something about her that I don't like. It's a hardness, a ruthlessness. Ted Heath was a very difficult man, but it was more acceptable in him. With Margaret, it's something in her that you can't relate to; you want to relate to her and expect to be able to as she is a woman. At home she's more sensitive and warm – but even there, this factor is still noticeable. You've got to be like that to get to where she is.'

Those who have had professional dealings with her are more explicit. During her time at the Department of Education, it is said, she never showed any softness or compassion. She herself once remarked that women politicians often combined in their own characters extreme toughness with concern for human problems, and she seems to combine within herself an extraordinary toughness with what have been described as 'Mothers' Union' attitudes. 'At moments I thought she was nothing but ice; I never felt there was any warmth at all,' said a colleague. 'But her manners were impeccable and included enormous generosity and consideration for others. Her manners meant she could believe you were appalling but would behave impeccably. But she is very, very – the only word I can find is vicious. She's a killer: she kills off ideas, reputations and people in her own mind. She had no compunction about liquidating the things she didn't like and in her own mind did just that; you were as good as dead. If you crossed her you would never get a job or good report but she would always seem to behave with impeccable good manners. She would not reveal personal animosity, but there was a good deal. She would classify whole sets of ideas and groups of people as "wet" or "pinko" for example. She makes up her mind about someone in ten seconds and then very rarely changes it. As soon as you open your mouth, you are categorised.'

Margaret Thatcher has the stoicism and resilience to withstand criticism – one of the hardest burdens to bear especially if one thinks, as Mrs Thatcher obviously does, that much of it is unfair and unwarranted.

While she was at the Department of Education, she came in for so much abuse that some newspapers dubbed her 'Britain's most unpopular woman'. She is remembered for abolishing free school milk to children under seven – but what is less widely known is that this was part of a legacy she inherited from Iain Macleod; and that she only carried out half of it. For Macleod had recommended that the Government should charge both for school milk and for libraries. Edward Heath was quite keen on both ideas, but Mrs Thatcher's reaction showed the powerful hold her upbringing still exercised over her. On no account would she ever charge for the use of libraries, she said; the very idea was anathema to her. After all, was it not through the Grantham library that her father had educated himself and his family and given Margaret her start in life? But milk was a different thing altogether; milk was welfare, not education, and didn't particularly matter. Alfred Roberts' benign influence on the nation's potential for self-education went, nevertheless, quite unremarked in the storm that followed the milk decision. The scale of the derision and abuse took her aback, although she never showed it; she was hurt but kept her cool in public and didn't duck the inevitable public confrontations.

Such a storm might well have proved too much for Shirley Williams, who has said that being the target for the nation's mud pies would be a powerful deterrent to becoming Prime Minister. Even more offensive to her would be the extent to which the abuse reflected on her family. Mrs Thatcher is obviously hurt by abuse, but seems to have developed a tough carapace to deal with it. In fact, the more criticism she gets, the more determined she appears to be to withstand it. She declared in 1972: 'I'm not hard; I'm frightfully soft. But I will not be hounded. I shall never be drawn anywhere against my will. And if people make a personal attack on me in the House, I can jolly well stick up for myself.' She also came to the comforting conclusion that women were fair game for criticism, which is a useful shield to wave in the face of whoever is launching an attack.

The milk affair was useful to her political development, since it was the first time she had been confronted by such hostility. Her problem when she arrived at the Education Ministry was that she was almost wholly unschooled in the realities of politics. Despite her interest in political life, developed in childhood and nurtured in the forum of university politics, despite her positions as spokesman on pensions, housing, the Treasury and power, and her period in the Shadow

Cabinet, she had no idea what politics were really about. It didn't occur to her that politics are about everything that affects a citizen's way of life: the food we eat, the house in which we live, the schools where we educate our children – whatever makes people happy or unhappy. And the basic problem of politics is that not everything can be achieved: choices have to be made, priorities have to be established. Mrs Thatcher's political career had exposed her to none of these things, and when she arrived at Education she brought with her a parcel of fixed views and very little else. She knew that the compulsory road to comprehensive education was anathema to her, and quickly took action to reverse that particular policy. But then she had to think very quickly about what other policies she wanted to pursue, and they turned out to be mainly concerned with how to distribute available money rather than with deeper issues of educational philosophy.

The policies that she espoused reflected the narrowness of her upbringing. Her lack of exposure to the wider world had produced a naivety and unworldliness that might be charming in other circumstances, but they were potentially alarming characteristics in a Minister of the Crown. It is said that she was profoundly puzzled by the Profumo affair in the sixties, when John Profumo, then War Minister, was at the centre of a scandal involving a prostitute who had links with the Russians. Mrs Thatcher simply couldn't understand the affair at all. It involved traits of character and patterns of behaviour quite unknown to her. The idea that people might pay large sums of money for the services of such prostitutes shocked the good housekeeper in her. This unworldliness did have its attractive side. She revealed herself to be an extremely honest person, even in her political dealings, and despised her colleagues if she thought they were not telling either individuals or the country the truth about what was going on. As one colleague ruefully remarked, if she was going to cut someone's political throat she would tell them she was going to do it. One of her fears was that some stain would be revealed on the sheets of her administration, that some skulduggery would be revealed in her department of which she would be ignorant until a scandal blew up.

But the corollary of such a lack of exposure to the real world was her narrowness of outlook. Her politics are based now, as they were then, on a fixed array of moral attitudes which depend on the philosophy of Samuel Smiles: that everyone is able to earn his own salvation. Although she has spoken admiringly of Disraeli, she is not a follower of his form of

Conservatism, his belief that Britain should be one nation and not divided into the rich and the poor. She believes that everyone can get what they want if they work hard – as she obviously believes she herself did. She takes no account of the fact that luck and privilege have to be recognised as playing their own part in success, and that these are factors which are not available to everyone equally. This narrowness displayed itself clearly in her policies at Education. She revealed a genuine belief that it was perfectly all right, even desirable, to spend money on the young. You couldn't go far wrong if you developed nursery education; it was right to give young children the opportunity to develop their interests and abilities.

But once those children grew older, and developed the capacity to take their own decisions and exercise their own free choice over their lives, her attitude changed. She was far less ready to spend money on the upper reaches of the education system because there she could see people taking money for the purposes of pleasure and not for the entirely worthwhile objective of furthering their education. Just as she was provided with the stimulus to learn in Grantham, so she would provide for the nation's children; but just as her family had to support her later on, so others would have to support their own.

Her colleagues also found that although she thought along establishment lines, she was extremely deferential to the establishment. One anecdote illustrates this attitude, and points up the difference in approach between Mrs Thatcher and Mrs Williams, who also served as Education Secretary. It is the custom when a new Secretary of State is installed for the most prominent people in the area of interest served by the Department to pay courtesy calls on the new Minister. When such calls were paid on Mrs Thatcher, her visitors were asked to wait in a room downstairs until her private secretary came to fetch them. But when she was told that waiting to see her were some university vice-chancellors—among the most prestigious bastions of the education establishment – she hurried downstairs to greet them herself and personally escort them up to her room. Yet Mrs Williams displayed a far more robust attitude towards these individuals, and was known to express as much impatience over their behaviour as she did over any other fractious group with which she had to deal.

Mrs Thatcher is an ambitious woman who obviously craved power, though this is not evident to all: to at least one devoted Conservative woman, a prominent worker in her own local constituency, it isn't obvious at all. To her, Mrs Thatcher was unmarked by the tawdry ambitions of mere politicians; she was possessed instead by an entirely altruistic zeal to do the best for her country. To illustrate her point, the woman related an anecdote about the 1978 conference of the party's Central Council, the governing body of the local associations, when Mrs Thatcher made an apparently stirring speech that received a tumultuous ovation. 'I slipped out of the back of the hall while the ovation was going on and waited until she came out. She emerged proudly and very much like the leader of the party, still in the aftermath of her speech. But as she came through the door she crumpled and looked just like a tired woman. Mrs Thatcher saw me and came over to me and although she didn't know me at all she took my hand in hers and put her hand on my shoulder and said, "I think it went all right, don't you?" At that point I thought, that's it, she really has no ambition for herself. She wants to become Prime Minister for the good of the country. She cares. When she talks, she gets down to what concerns me, what the future is going to be for my children and grandchildren; it's not something that male politicians ever do.'

What are we to make of this anecdote? Does it tell us that the constituency woman had been totally fooled, and that because she had seen proof that her leader was human, with traits with which she could identify, she had concluded wrongly that her motives were untarnished by personal ambition? Or does it tell us more about Mrs Thatcher? It has been suggested by several people, themselves untouched by the idolatry of this particular party worker, that women politicians do have a conception of power that is different from that of their male colleagues. Men, the theory goes, want power for its own sake, want to be leader of the pack. Women want it because with it they can change society and improve the lot of their fellows.

This distinction seems to be as specious and simplistic as the theory that Mrs Thatcher is untouched by personal ambition. She does undoubtedly have a clear idea of how she wants British society to be altered; she is undoubtedly under the impression that the measures she has set in train are necessary to arrest the country's decline and make it great again. But although these convictions are extremely noticeable in her—partly, at least, because they conflict with the consensus politics of more than twenty years—the desire to change society is the very stuff of politics and quite inseparable from the desire to fulfil personal ambition. Barbara Castle recognised that the distinction could not be made. 'Ambitious? It's very difficult of course to distinguish honestly in oneself between ambition for the cause of service and ambition for yourself, to know where the ego takes over. You can't keep going unless you believe that your personal contribution to the cause matters and so it is important to maximise that contribution. All causes are made up of a large number of very active egos and anyone who tells you differently is wrong. But you must have a check on yourself from outside to stop your ego from misleading you. I certainly admit that I tend to be egocentric; I've a strong capacity for concentration and that makes me go about almost in a dream world when there's a job to do. I find it unbearable to leave anything half-mastered; it's the perfectionist in me, and unless I'm careful this becomes self-indulgence.' Yet she too recoiled from the idea that what she wanted was power; she would rather call it public responsibility. And responsibility was what she thrived on; making decisions and then standing up and accounting for them publicly was for her the stimulation of life. Small wonder, then, that at the age of sixty-seven she started a new career in European politics.

All these women have quite different attitudes towards their public image. Shirley Williams appears to be quite careless of her own, yet has apparently managed to produce one that camouflages part of her character. She comes across as a politician of total integrity, which she undoubtedly is; even her opponents grant her that. She gives the impression of having a mature perspective on life in which her statements of belief are all worked out in a wider context which gives her a coherent philosophy. Interviews with her are rarely able to dwell on personal details of her own life, but are soon removed to the more abstract intellectual plane of her beliefs, principles and ideas. She is noted for a corresponding impatience with the trivial business of her physical appearance. Even at Oxford she was described as a 'Shetland pony', and Lady Astor displayed both rudeness and an absence of political prescience when she told her, 'You will never get on in politics, my dear, with that hair.'

She has a considerable amount of personal charm, and flatters those who talk to her by listening intently to what they have to say and thinking about the points they have made, even if she then knocks them down. Her principled honesty means that everyone seems to love her, even her political enemies. *The Times,* which on 4 June 1970 tipped her to become Prime Minister, was positively eulogistic about her: 'If one had to pick a single Labour M.P. in whose social conscience one could trust it would be Mrs Shirley Williams. It is relatively easy to enter politics with a social conscience but quite a bit more difficult to retain and develop it in full knowledge of what society can be like in its bad moments. It is also not easy to be a successful woman politician. The pressures are very intense and they are pressures which can make a woman unattractively aggressive in order to show that she can't be bettered by men. Shirley Williams is not a bit like that. She is one of those rare women who could become Prime Minister (and perhaps should) without losing a scrap of her good nature and charm and without thinking any the better of herself for it.'

Even the *Daily Mail* was impressed by the stand she took over the Common Market, when she overrode the Prime Minister's veto in 1974 to make a courageous personal statement. If the referendum vote on Europe went against British membership, she said, she would not wish to remain in active politics, and if a Labour Cabinet recommended such a vote she would resign from it. The *Mail* enthused on 6 September 1974: 'The directness of Mrs Williams' approach does not surprise those who know her. She is, in the best sense of the word, a simple person. She has little guile, or malice, and is possessed of an obvious desire to do the decent thing by her fellow citizens. She is the sort of person – albeit unusually intelligent and articulate – whom one finds self-effacingly helping a hundred good causes in parishes and villages up and down the country.'

But this image, and the universal affection it inspires, has riled some of her women colleagues in the House of Commons. This can possibly be partly explained away as jealousy, but the resentment has also arisen because the image doesn't present the whole truth. It presents her as such a soft personality that one wonders how she ever got so near to the top of the political tree. But underneath the sympathetic exterior, Mrs Williams is a hard and polished political operator. If Mrs Thatcher is the Wimbledon tennis champion, punching home her shots with determination and in the full glare of public opinion, Shirley Williams is the chess player, manoeuvring with great subtlety and intelligence but with her eye equally on a final goal. Like Mrs Thatcher, she believes passionately in her own vision of society; like Mrs Thatcher, she desires power to bring it about. One man who dealt with her as Education Secretary remarked: 'She was an adept politician, determined although never ruthless. Underneath the charm there was quite a sharp thrust; sometimes little sharp points emerged and then would be buried again.'

By way of complete contrast with Mrs Williams, Barbara Castle was always most concerned about her physical appearance, a concern which did not diminish as she grew older. The quality of her intellect and the incisiveness of her mind commanded considerable respect; Harold Wilson's remark that Barbara was 'the best man in my Cabinet' has been repeated so often that its patronising message has now passed into the realms of cliché. But she was always regarded, even among her friends, as someone who was not above resorting to her femininity to get her own way. Such an assessment does, I think, sometimes reflect more on the people who make it than on the truth of the observation. For they appear to have confused certain obvious characteristics of Mrs Castle – her showmanship, her immaculate grooming, her tenacity – with femininity. Those who dislike her draw attention to the less amenable side of her personality in the same breath as the fact that she is a woman – and in so doing probably reveal more about their own prejudices than they do about Mrs Castle herself.

Not that she has ever been afraid of her femininity. She told Susan Barnes in the *Sun* on 24 January 1966: 'I'll tell you why I think it makes me a better politician not to erase my femininity. The secret really in public life is to be a person. For some reason – some of it through their cramping themselves with self-restraint – women often emerge as admirable administrators but not as people. You've got to be yourself. You've almost got to defy the public: "That's me. Take me or leave me."' But at the same time as she revelled in being a woman, she insisted that she never made any capital out of it. She told Kenneth Harris in the *Observer* on 5 October 1969: 'I'm a woman everywhere and all the time. I don't fight against being a woman. I like it. I love being a woman. I think the only really distinctive contribution women should be expected to make in political life is to get into politics and when in politics behave as naturally and unselfconsciously as possible. I've never been as emotional in my public life as some male politicians I know. Certainly I have never consciously exploited the fact that I am a woman, I wouldn't dare to try that even if I knew how to. I have too much respect for my male colleagues to think they would be particularly impressed.'

But the image that has been put across in the press is quite different. Paul Johnson, then editor of the *New Statesman*, wrote in the *Daily Mirror* on 26 July 1968 that she was not above using 'feminine wiles' when necessary. He accused her of using tears to get her own way when logical persuasion had failed – a charge she vehemently denied – and said that she had once told him how she could cajole the whips: 'If I want to get out of a vote and present all kinds of unanswerable arguments to my whip he won't listen. But if I put my head on his shoulder and say, Oh Whippy, would you do me a favour, he gives way immediately. It's disgusting.' Such stories have more than a whiff of the apocryphal about them, and have undoubtedly helped shroud Mrs Castle in myth. Nevertheless, she did possess a powerful personality, a flair for directing the spotlights on to herself and a particular talent for getting the things she wanted done.

The main reason for this, however, was that she was extraordinarily tenacious: she never gave up, and simply wore the opposition down. It is said that on the issue of child benefit, which she was trying to push through an unwilling Cabinet and an even more hostile Treasury, she telephoned Joel Barnett, the Chief Secretary to the Treasury, while he was digging his garden at home, and bent his ear about the merits of the scheme. His mind was still half engrossed in the problem of weeding his cabbages or whatever, so he agreed with her in order to get back to his gardening. She was renowned for her battles in Cabinet and on the party's National Executive Committee, which she won by having first done her homework and then refusing to give up the fight. No 'feminine wiles' were necessary for this; it simply required a particular kind of personality. But those who dislike the tactics she used tend to slot her into feminine stereotypes: hence her tenacity becomes 'nagging' or 'bossiness'.

One man who observed both Mrs Castle and Mrs Williams on the N.E.C. told me that Mrs Castle's tactics could only have been employed by a woman. 'She has long nails and uses them,' he said. 'She's a thoroughly aggressive woman, determined to get her own way. It's all above board with her – you never see her working behind anyone's back, but she fights in her corner with more determination than most people.' The bear-garden politics of the N.E.C., he said, suited her temperament far more than they did Shirley Williams. 'There's not a moment in time when Barbara says, I've lost, and gives in. One knows before Barbara starts that she is determined to win the discussion. Shirley has throw-away lines; she will say, this is government policy, like it or lump it. Barbara comes in because she wants to win. Shirley comes in and wants to put a point of view. Having expressed it, the other participants can put their views. She's more detached than other people on the N.E.C. But Barbara will resort to personal abuse. Most people have a set-piece argument in debate. Barbara is prepared to use any argument at any time to win it. She terrorises the men. People give in so as to end the argument. In the end the arguments become so vicious she defeats her opponents who say, I've had enough. They would rather give away their point than be involved any more in the argument. Shirley, on the other hand, wants her side to be triumphant but there's a little bit of the girl guide in her; it must be honest and above board, and arguments must be won fairly and squarely. Her contributions to debates are better than most people's. But I doubt very much if they are listened to as much as Barbara's.'

One can detect, beneath the prejudices of this man's opinion, a kernel of truth: Mrs Castle is a tenacious woman and Mrs Williams is more detached. But his comments are also interesting because they reveal the attitudes of at least one of the men with whom these women have to deal in their political lives, and through whose opinions their public images are filtered. This man is used to an all-male environment and does not know how to cope with the presence of women on the N.E.C. – all of whom, he maintains, with the exception of Joan Lestor, argue 'like women'. When pressed to explain exactly what he means, he strokes his chin and looks at the ceiling and confesses he cannot quite put his finger on it, but it's definitely something different, although he knows he shouldn't be saying this.

Of all three women, it is Mrs Thatcher who has most noticeably worked at her image, and has taken advice on how to change it in order to broaden her electoral appeal. It was not suprising that she should wish to do this; Denis Healey's jibe, that she was the 'La Pasionara of middle-class privilege', struck home, despite its unpleasant sexist overtones. Nevertheless, the degree of slickness and sophistication with which she allowed herself to be packaged before the 1979 election was breathtaking. Just like the way in which presidents of the United States are sold to the public, the process demeaned and trivialised her but achieved its desired end. For that she won the admiration of Lady Falkender, who is certain, as someone who helped mastermind some of Harold Wilson's more publicised election stunts, that such gimmicks are the only way to win elections.

The problem, in publicity terms, was fairly straightforward. The product to be marketed was a woman who had taken some pains in the past to translate the ordinary, commonplace characteristics of her background into a middle-class accent, appearance and values. The trouble was that she had been too successful in the process and was now seen to be too distant from the very sort of people she prided herself on having come from. A perfect illustration of this was provided by the tale of Mrs Thatcher's visit to a school science class, where the children came from fairly rough working-class homes. They were doing an experiment using spoons made of some cheap alloy. Mrs Thatcher came in, picked up one of the spoons, and said, 'These, of course, are not made from silver like the ones you have at home.'

Her advisers were nervous that, with her habit of saying what she thought without much concern for the consequences, she might make a blunder which would cost her the election. Additionally, her general image was perceived as too remote. So a campaign was launched which provided her with the maximum of a certain kind of exposure to publicity, with the minimum of exposure of any other kind. The exposure that she went in for can only be described as stunts for the benefit of the television cameras and the press photographers. Almost every night, it seemed, there on the television news was the woman who was laying claim to be Prime Minister engaged in a series of ever more extraordinary and absurd public relations gimmicks. She engaged in a tea-tasting exercise; we saw the woman who was shortly going to decide the fate of Britain's economy sip delicately from spoons and then screw up her face in disgust. She boxed chocolates, monitored her heart, wielded brooms, stitched cloth, embraced a new-born calf in a field. At that point, the stunts appeared to degenerate into self-parody. With a combination of extreme cynicism and embarrassing honesty, she declared, as she marshalled the travelling circus of observers out of the way of the cameras: 'It's not for me, it's for the photographers; they're the important people in this campaign.' It seemed impossible to believe that anyone watching this American-style razmatazz could have been deceived for one moment. But it self-evidently did not spoil Mrs Thatcher's chance of success – and Lady Falkender remarked to me that she was not surprised. Anything that made Mrs Thatcher more human and approachable was obviously good public relations, she said. And if people laughed and exclaimed over the stunts so much the better; it meant that Mrs Thatcher had at least descended from her Dresden china pedestal.

At the same time, her physical appearance changed. The hair style softened; she was told to speak more slowly and closer to the microphone so that the tone of her voice was mellowed; her clothes changed from affluent suburban to chic executive. The stunts, shopping expeditions and set-piece speeches were all exploited to their full publicity potential. But at the same time, Mrs Thatcher gave hardly any interviews. She is known to dislike television, where she tends to appear tense and stilted, but she is also reluctant to give interviews to journalists who are unlikely to be sympathetic. First blood of the election campaign went to Mr Callaghan when he publicly challenged Mrs Thatcher to a debate on television about the issues of the election. Mrs Thatcher's refusal to take part was all the more noticeable against the background of her frequent appearances in gimmicky situations. And as the election campaign wore on, the absence of any serious interviewing of the Leader of the Opposition became more pronounced. This coyness was not confined to the election period. I made a number of attempts to see Mrs Thatcher before, during and after the election, but met with no success. Other writers and journalists have experienced similar difficulties with her which they have not encountered with other politicians.

Yet in the interviews she has given, the remarkable thing is that she is more than happy to present herself as Mrs Average Housewife, an aspect one would have thought she would be at pains to play down because of the trivialising effect this has on her image. In the past she has emphasised that she wants to be regarded as a politician, not a woman politician, a desire one would expect of someone with aspirations to the highest offices of state. One would have thought therefore that Mrs Thatcher would be profoundly irritated by the patronising treatment of her in the press. Apparently not – for she has revealed a marked enthusiasm for reducing herself to the level of the trivial.

Take, for example, the extended interviews she granted to Kenneth Harris of the *Observer* in both October 1975 and February 1978. In the earlier one, the following points were put to her: 'You are always beautifully dressed, and your hair is always lovely. Do you, as is said of some women, dress for men? And what's your favourite colour?' Could one imagine, for example, Denis Healey or Keith Joseph being asked similar questions – and then replying, as Mrs Thatcher did, that they dressed to look well turned out and that their favourite colour was turquoise? In the later interview, she took it even further, and emphasised, as she has always been keen to do, the element of the housewife in her and the extent to which she can therefore identify with the women of the country and they with her. On 18 February 1978 she said, 'I *do* my own shopping, I *do* know what women have to put up with, I know what it's like to run a home and job . . . Men have a great regard for their wives' perceptive comments. And they know that women are not only more practical, but they are not so much concerned with pernickety detail.' She has gone out of her way to make this sort of point. In an interview in *Woman's World* magazine in October 1978 she said: 'Just think, the women of this country have never had a Prime Minister who knew the things that they knew: never, never. And the things that we know are very different from what men know. Things like doing your budget every week and actually having the running of a house under your control. You know that certain things have got to be done: the washing, the shirts have got to be ironed, what it's like to go down to the shops and make your housekeeping stretch.'

It is not that this image of herself is a false one. Civil servants at the Department of Education, when it was based in premises in Mayfair, were often amazed by the way Mrs Thatcher balanced her overriding commitment to the domestic details of her life with the tough political operator in her personality. The tale is told of how, with a few minutes to go to an 11 a.m. Cabinet meeting, she would suddenly say to the civil servants briefing her on crucial policy issues that she had to dash down to the butcher's in nearby Shepherd Market before it closed to buy bacon for Denis, her husband. They would protest that there were a number of people who could perform this chore for her, and that surely she had higher calls on her time, but no, she had to go and buy it personally because only she knew what Denis liked. The absurd stunts in which the Leader of the Opposition did her shopping in the local grocer's surrounded by an armada of cameramen were putting over an image to win votes, but they also contained an element of truth.

Mrs Thatcher is fond of describing herself as a 'conviction politician' – as if this distinguishes her from the rabble of those who are in politics with less honourable purposes in mind. In fact, Mrs Williams and Mrs Castle are also 'conviction politicians'; they believe strongly in certain principles that they wish to see put into practice. The difference between them and Mrs Thatcher is that both Mrs Williams and Mrs Castle know that politics represent the art of the possible, and compromises must be made. There are signs that Mrs Thatcher is beginning to recognise this, but only very slowly. For her mind, although undoubtedly as sharp as any, runs on rigid intellectual tramlines and is not receptive to alternative points of view. Those who have worked with her say that she cannot brook opposition.

One person from the education world said that she had a brittle intellect; she repeated superficial, glib answers but never thought very deeply about things, in contrast to Shirley Williams who thought deeply about everything and had the gift of seeing into the heart of a problem the instant it was put to her. 'You felt that when you were arguing with Margaret you were both starting from preconceived frameworks. You always felt that you were parading the arguments and you knew before you went in that you would never get any movement from her. With Shirley, you got the impression that she listened carefully and was prepared to argue on rather deeper grounds.' Mrs Thatcher would, in argument, pick opponents up on small points and then insist on proving them wrong. People emerged from meetings with her scratching their heads and saying that all they seemed to be doing was hitting the ball into their own goal. Another said: 'She was the absolute stereotype of the clever sixth-form girl who reads chemistry; she was a marvellous examination candidate because she could read and remember almost anything. She sorted all the information out into drawers in her mind. But there's a huge gap between being clever and being wise. She was not wise. She lacked that vital other dimension: imagination. She had a totally unoriginal mind.'

This narrow intellectual approach is reflected in Mrs Thatcher's policies, in which apparently logical deductions are made from fundamental convictions. She believes that immigration should stop, and gave an election commitment to that end. Hence, Britain could not accept the Vietnamese refugees because this would count as immigration. The fact that the plight of the refugees raised entirely different questions from Britain's legal and moral responsibilities towards immigrants from Asia did not seem to occur to her. In the event, she was persuaded that Britain could and should step up the quota of refugees it was prepared to take in. Similarly, she was persuaded away from her initial desire to recognise the Muzorewa regime in Zimbabwe-Rhodesia and end sanctions as fast as possible. This desire followed from the premise that the situation in Rhodesia had changed: it now had a black African as its Prime Minister; ergo, everyone should be satisfied and Britain should recognise Rhodesia as legally independent. She had to be forced to concede, through the pressures of international diplomacy and the influence of Lord Carrington, that this superficial impression may not have been the whole truth, and that in politics it is not always possible to cut a swathe of policy regardless of who might be standing in the way.

The pragmatic realities of politics were something that Barbara Castle came to understand well, despite her reputation as a rebel on the left of the Labour Party. She had just as much conviction, and courage to back her principles, as Margaret Thatcher. She had made her Parliamentary reputation with blazing speeches on Cyprus, the Hola refugee camp in Kenya and German rearmament, in which she had pushed political expediency to one side; yet she was later responsible for *In Place of Strife*, in which she appeared to be taking on her former allies on the left, and still later in her career for the compromise over the issue of pay beds in health service hospitals. Had she changed? Or was she simply putting into practice a lesson she had been taught years before in Bradford?

The row over *In Place of Strife*, her White Paper on industrial relations, centred around three of its proposals: that Ministers could enforce a 28-day 'conciliation pause', impose settlements in multi-union disputes, and insist on ballots being held before strikes. The ensuing row almost engulfed the Labour Party and ended in a face-saving compromise in the shape of an undertaking from the T.U.C. to take steps to encourage strikers to return to work. This was the first time that Mrs Castle, who was now officially termed First Secretary and Secretary of State for Employment and Productivity, had moved away from her left-wing principles. Or had she? She said in 1969: 'To me, politics has always been a question of the under-equipped equipping themselves to influence their environment, to mould it, to get on top of it . . . This moulding of the environment . . . you can't have it for everybody else and not have it for such important sectors of society as prices and incomes and trade unions' accountability. Those who seek to oppose me understand this point of view and still regard me as a socialist and we can agree about it in perfect mutual respect which is really rather marvellous. But what would hurt me would be if they said that Barbara had ceased to be a socialist and a left-winger, therefore, she should be removed from the Executive. They don't say that.'

Whether or not she had shifted her political position in putting the proposals forward, she undoubtedly suffered a humiliating defeat over them. But she did not resign; when it came to the crunch, political survival was more important to her. She appeared to accept not just that some battles were going to be lost, but that when it came to translating ideals into practice reality had an awkward tendency to intrude. She told Kenneth Harris of the *Observer* on 28 August 1969 that she had learned the cost of action in Bradford. 'My father used to say it always cost something to turn theory into action and how important it was to face the cost and pay the price. Ideals are your own, all your own, and have perfect integrity so long as you do nothing about them. Once you act, you leave the splendid simplicity of your own version of truth and find that it has its own contradictions and ironies at the heart of it. It is not a question of being forced to compromise. I hate that word; it's misleading. It suggests that truth lies somewhere halfway between my concept of society and my opponent's. It's rather that one discovers the cost of achieving one's own vision and that the only soft option is not to act.'

Shirley Williams fell halfway between the realism of Mrs Castle and the dogmatism of Mrs Thatcher. She understood that politics were full of hard choices, but she would not cut her losses in the same way as Mrs Castle was known to do. On the issue of Europe, for example, if the referendum result had not gone her way Mrs Williams would have resigned from active politics. After her defeat at the polls she was expected to try to return to Parliament before long, but her involvement in active politics will undoubtedly depend on the way the Labour Party develops. If it were to be led by someone who she thought would lead it in a totally wrong direction, she would probably not return. This is undoubtedly because she is a woman of strong principles, but it is a position also made possible by her sense of detachment from the political arena, maintained even while she was in the very thick of it.

Before she came into Parliament in 1964 she was torn between politics and journalism, uncertain whether she wanted to become an M.P. And all the way through her career in the House of Commons she was painfully aware of the sacrifices she was having to make in her personal life. She was conscious that she had hardly any time for family, for listening to music or going to the theatre, for spending time with friends and people outside politics. A radio programme on which she appeared with Mrs Thatcher in 1973 revealed the difference in their commitment to politics. Mrs Thatcher said: 'Politics gets into your bloodstream. I would do everything over again; I love it in spite of all the difficulties and all the criticism.' But although Mrs Williams agreed that politics were exciting and worthwhile, she was far more equivocal: 'I'm now more conscious of the price one has to pay in terms of all the other things that you can't do – and will never be able to do now – and that's something of a regret to me.'

Yet one feels that her disenchantment went deeper than frustration at not being able to do everything, and struck at the very heart of Parliamentary politics. As early as 1965, she wrote in a bitterly critical article in the *Observer*: 'There's a kind of stoical satisfaction in sitting up all night, drinking tea and aimlessly gossiping and letting it be known that one has been through the night watch. And then one is suddenly aware that this is a crazy ritual sacrifice . . . In the long nights in the great neo-Gothic palace most of us realise how cut off we are from the city outside. You lose touch. The peculiar parliamentary game with its unwritten customs and its tyrannical traditions is part of a private world . . . After watching the sad little procession of sick members, the stretchers and the beds made up in the Ministers' rooms for those unable even to walk, one feels that the private game has gone on too long and has been ludicrously savage. At its least edifying, the House of Commons is like a minor boys' public school. And it is usually at its least edifying on the "great occasions". The famous treble of censure debates intended as a coda to the whole system were simply a waste of time. We knew it all – the formal denunciation – 13 wasted years and a deficit versus 10 wasted months and a crisis of confidence. The backbenchers duly bayed and shouted as they were expected to do. The front benchers equally duly arraigned and denounced and that was expected too. Of course there were genuine moments of drama: the Prime Minister's fantastic performance on Thursday when Labour morale was low; Edward Heath, white-knuckled and furious on Monday, for once losing his normal tense composure. In the end, however, the great occasions may reveal something about men but they reveal virtually nothing about the issues . . . The conventional geography of politics doesn't fit these new men. We are soldiers in a mock battle who know that, close by, a real battle is raging: the struggle for Britain's economic survival.'

Her friends say that in a way she was extremely relieved to have lost her seat in the 1979 election. She was getting very fed up with life as a Minister, with politics generally and with the Labour Party in particular. She was used over and over again as the acceptable face of Government policy, to be displayed to the electorate and, more onerously, to the Labour Party's National Executive Committee, where she was expected to defend and explain the Government's policies. She was unhappy about the way the Government seemed constantly to be looking over its shoulder at the N.E.C. on the issue of Europe and modifying its stand accordingly – or so it appeared to her. It wasn't so much an intellectual strain; she was, after all, known to be one of the fastest readers of a

Government brief. It was more an emotional debilitation caused by having so much of her life consumed by the pressures of office – and she took both her departmental duties and membership of the Cabinet extremely seriously.

She and Mrs Thatcher have two things in common: phenomenal energy and an incapacity to delegate. Mrs Williams' former husband, Professor Bernard Williams, once described her as 'a power house, crunching everywhere at a mass of material'. She is said to possess remarkable powers of recovery which enable her to recharge herself moments after appearing exhausted and defeated. Mrs Thatcher, similarly, is renowned for her ability to survive on very little sleep and for the speed and thoroughness with which she works at her material. One union leader who had had dealings with both of them said that they both worked in a constant flurry of activity; neither turned up to meetings on time, and they would often leave such meetings before the actual business was finished in order to hurry off to another. Neither paced herself properly, and neither could delegate; nor could they distinguish between urgent matters, which they had to deal with themselves, and the points of detail, which could have been left to their civil servants.

The story is told of Shirley Williams that soon after her arrival at the Home Office as Minister of State, with responsibility for the prison service, she was handed a bundle of prisoners' petitions. Usually such petitions are dealt with in a cursory way by the Minister, who then leaves it to the civil servants to decide what to do with them. Mrs Williams, however, insisted on looking at all of them, and her interest was caught by one from a prisoner who was asking to be let out to visit the dentist. The civil servants took the view that this man had used visits to the dentist on a number of occasions in the past as a ruse to have a trip away from the prison. The prison authorities had gone along with it, but now the excuse was wearing thin and they had lost patience. They advised Mrs Williams that she should therefore turn the petition down. But she took home the man's file containing all his previous petitions, spread them all out on her kitchen floor, studied the history of the affair, and decided that as it wouldn't cost that much he should be allowed out to the dentist just one more time. Incidents like this both amused and exasperated her civil servants, who were bowled over by her charm and intelligence but infuriated by her incapacity to delegate.

Mrs Thatcher's similar incapacity is, however, worrying some observers, especially now that she is Prime Minister. She likes to do everything herself; civil servants have been astonished by the fact that she has travelled personally to the Treasury to chair a Cabinet finance committee, an unprecedented display of personal control. She could do this sort of thing at Education, and in Shadow Cabinet, said one observer, but she can't do it indefinitely as Prime Minister. She has phenomenal energy, but something eventually has to give, especially if there is some sort of crisis. The kind of pressure that she's under now will otherwise provoke a crisis in her. And if she is seen to fail as Prime Minister, she will not only ruin her own political career, but will set back the advancement of women in politics. Now that she is settled in 10 Downing Street, there is less attention paid to the fact that she is a woman than to her remarkable personality and the policies she has set in train. But if she fails, there can be no doubt that her sex will be used as a weapon against her; as she herself has remarked, women are not afforded a second chance. Mrs Thatcher, Mrs Williams and Mrs Castle are all outstanding politicians, who rose to positions of power through their own attributes. But the ultimate fragility of their position serves as a reminder that apart from the roles they have played in the wider political scene, they are also leading players in the intriguing story of the fight by women for political equality.

2 *The Battle for Westminster*

IF social progress can be measured by the way a society treats its women members, then judging by the number of its women M.P.s Britain has started to move backwards. Only nineteen women were elected M.P.s in the 1979 general election, the smallest total since 1951 when seventeen were elected and fewer than the twenty-four elected in the Labour landslide of 1945. Even in 1929, at the first general election after the introduction of full female suffrage, fourteen women were elected, two of whom were appointed to ministerial posts. There were more women Ministers in Clement Attlee's Government in 1945 than were appointed by Margaret Thatcher in 1979 – four in 1945, compared with three in 1979. These startling figures show that statistically women Members of Parliament are just as freakish as they were fifty years ago; although the number of women contesting seats has risen from seventeen in 1918 to 206 in 1979, the numbers elected have never exceeded 5 per cent of the total. The gentlemen's club at the Palace of Westminster has remained a largely male preserve, prepared to tolerate women among its ranks provided there are not too many of them.

When Mrs Thatcher became Prime Minister, the election that gave her victory marked a drop in the number of women M.P.s from the total of twenty-seven who had been elected in October 1974. It was a most ironic and frustrating twist to an election that was hailed all over the world as historic because it had put the first woman into Number Ten.

Symbolically, women had finally made it to the top of the political ladder; realistically, the cause of equality for women in politics had slithered down the snake again. In fact, the whole history of the fight for women's democratic rights has been punctuated by irony and paradox; it is the story of how an oppressed majority was thwarted time and again in its struggle for equal rights by a minority who feared an erosion of its power. Eventually a stalemate was reached, which still shows no sign of being broken.

The fight for women's representation in Parliament was the logical extension of the earlier battle for women's suffrage; indeed, one of the reasons for the determined opposition to giving women the vote was that men perceived that representation at Westminster would inevitably follow. The suffragist movement really got under way in the second half of the nineteenth century, although political consciousness among women dated back at least as far as 1792 when Mary Wollstonecraft published *A Vindication of the Rights of Women*. Throughout the early part of the nineteenth century, women were afforded some political activity through the Anti-Corn Law League and the Birmingham Political Union, which gave rise to the subsidiary Women's Political Association. In 1865 the suffragist movement received its biggest fillip with the election to Parliament of John Stuart Mill, a supporter of their cause, who proposed a suffrage Bill two years later. Between 1870 and 1900, a suffrage Bill was proposed in every Parliamentary session except one, but to no avail.

By the turn of the century, middle-class women were becoming doctors and nurses and working-class women were starting to work in offices and factories. In 1907 women became eligible to vote and stand in local government elections. Meanwhile, the anti-suffrage lobby stood firm. The Liberal Party was, among the rank and file at least, sympathetic to the idea of women's suffrage but its leaders were against it, probably because they were worried that women of property, if given the vote, would use it to back the Conservatives. The Labour Party was equivocal: although it had always supported universal franchise, it was disinclined to ally itself with a movement that consisted largely of middle and upper-class women and which was pressing to extend the franchise to people of property.

Mr Gladstone, leader of the Liberal Party, had shocked many by his anti-suffrage stand. On 11 April 1892 he wrote to Mr Samuel Smith: 'The woman's vote carries with it, whether by the same Bill or by a consequent Bill, the woman's seat in Parliament . . . If the woman's vote carries with it the woman's seat, have we at this point reached our terminus and found a standing ground which we can in reason and in justice regard as final? Capacity to sit in the House of Commons now legally and practically draws in its train capacity to fill every office in the state . . . I think it impossible to deny that there have been and are women individually fit for any public office however masculine its character, just as there are persons under the age of 21 better fitted than many of those beyond it for the discharge of the duties of full citizenship. In neither case does the argument derived from exceptional instances seem to justify the abolition of the general rule . . . I am not without the fear lest beginning with the state we should eventually be found to have intruded into what is yet more fundamental and more sacred, the precinct of the family, and should dislocate or injuriously modify the relations of domestic life.'

Nor were men alone in their opposition to women's suffrage. In June 1889 a letter signed by 104 women in the periodical the *Nineteenth Century* said: 'The quickness to feel, the willingness to lay aside prudential considerations in a right cause, which are among the peculiar excellencies of women, are in their right place when they are used to influence the more highly trained and developed judgement of men. But if this quickness of feeling could be immediately and directly translated into public action, in matters of vast and complicated political import, the risks of politics would be enormously increased and what is now a national blessing might easily become a national calamity.' While in 1909 Mr Arthur Gronno wrote in a pamphlet published by the Manchester branch of the Women's National Anti-Suffrage League: 'To give votes to women with . . . its corollary, the woman M.P., would lower the quality of our legislation, would increase the number of capricious, emotional and meddlesome laws and would therefore in many cases bring the law into contempt and render it a dead letter.'

In 1910, an all-party committee of M.P.s drafted a conciliation Bill which would have given the vote to married women property holders. It was opposed by Mr Lloyd George, Chancellor of the Exchequer, and failed. It was rewritten and re-submitted in 1911 and in 1912 but failed again both times. However, the suffragist movement had taken a more militant form after the formation in 1903 of Mrs Emmeline Pankhurst's Women's Social and Political Union, which decided that deeds, not words, were the only way to win the vote for women. From 1905, when

Christabel Pankhurst and Annie Kenny were imprisoned after a demonstration at Manchester Free Trade Hall, until the First World War, militant suffragettes mounted a campaign of civil disobedience in which they suffered imprisonment, brutality and even death.

With the advent of war, the suffragettes declared an amnesty and devoted themselves to the war effort. The immense admiration for women generated by the work they did during the war, the social changes and the size of support for the National Union of Women's Suffrage Societies, meant that by the end of the war the women's claim to the vote had become overwhelming. On 6 February 1918 the Representation of the People Act, granting the vote to women of thirty and over who were householders or who were married to householders, received the Royal Assent. Later that year, with a general election drawing near, the coalition government decided to put the issue of women's representation in Parliament to a free vote. On 23 October 1918, *Hansard* records that Mr Herbert Samuel, Liberal M.P. for Cleveland, proposed that a Bill should be passed to allow women to become M.P.s. He argued, with considerable insight, that it was likely that too few women would be elected to Parliament rather than too many. Women should be able to become M.P.s at twenty-one, he said, since the voting age qualification of thirty had only been imposed on women voters temporarily so that they should not outnumber men in the immediate post war period. There was hardly any opposition to the motion; Mr Asquith, who had opposed women's suffrage, grudgingly told the House: 'You have the camel; you ought not to strain at the gnat.' The House voted for the motion by 274 votes to twenty-five; on 31 October the Parliament (Qualification of Women) Bill was presented; it was rushed through in three weeks and received the Royal Assent on the day Parliament was prorogued. There was now the absurd possibility that a woman of twenty-one could become an M.P. nine years before she was entitled to exercise her democratic rights through the ballot box.

There was then, in the immediate aftermath of the war, a confusing mêlée as candidates jostled for seats, and in this inauspicious rush seventeen women were selected out of 1,623 candidates. Pamela Brookes, in her book *Women at Westminster*, has chronicled the identities of these seventeen pioneers. The Labour and Liberal Parties put up four women each, the Conservatives put up one, and there were eight others. Labour put forward Miss Mary Macarthur, a legendary woman who had become secretary of the Women's Trade Union League. Also fighting for Labour was Mrs Emmeline Pethick Lawrence, a militant suffragette; Mrs Charlotte Despard, another famous suffragette who was seventy-four at the time of the election; and Mrs H.M. Mackenzie, a professor of education. The Liberals put up Mrs Marjorie Corbett Ashby, a Cambridge graduate who was fighting Neville Chamberlain; Miss Alison Garland, known as the 'Lloyd George in petticoats'; Mrs J. McEwan, the wife of a city businessman; and Miss Violet Markham, who had been an anti-suffragist until the war. The best known of the Independents was Miss Christabel Pankhurst, daughter of Emmeline, who represented the Women's Party, the only attempt to ensure a completely separate route for women into Parliament. The others included two suffragettes, a leading member of the Women's Freedom League, a feminist headmistress and a Cambridge graduate who had published a novel at the age of eighteen and who had been a key worker in the N.U.W.S.S. There were also two Sinn Fein candidates, Miss Winifred Carney and Countess Markievicz, who intended not to take their seats if elected.

This, of course, provided the supreme irony of the 1918 election, because Constance Markievicz was the only woman to be elected. Condemned to death for her part in the Easter Rising, a sentence later commuted to penal servitude for life, she was released under an amnesty in 1917 but re-imprisoned in May 1918. As a result, she contested the election from her cell in Holloway prison. For her, home rule was more important than women's rights. She received a letter from Lloyd George summoning her to attend the opening of Parliament, but although she was released from Holloway a few months later she never took her seat. It must have been a peculiarly galling twist of fate for the committed feminists who had fought the election and who had all failed in their attempt to get to Westminster.

This ironic anti-climax was followed by an equally ironic success, when the American-born Nancy Astor, who had never campaigned for women's rights, became the first woman to take her seat in the House of Commons. In 1919 the death of his father meant that Waldorf Astor, the Conservative M.P. for Plymouth, Sutton, succeeded to his place in the House of Lords. He suggested that his wife, Nancy, should stand in his place, a suggestion accepted by the party since Lady Astor was popular and talented, with a considerable wit and a gift for sparkling repartee. She was duly elected, and made her maiden speech about one of her pet causes, the evils of drink. Vera Brittain, in her book *Lady into Woman*, reported Lady Astor as saying: 'Men whom I had known for years would not speak to me if they passed me in the corridors. They said I would not last six months. But I stuck it out.' She saw her role in Parliament both as representing her constituency and as a spokeswoman for the women and children of the country, a dual role that many women M.P.s still acknowledge.

In 1921, Lady Astor was joined by a second woman M.P., also elected at a by-election in her husband's constituency. Mr Tom Wintringham, the Liberal M.P. for Louth in Lincolnshire, died and his widow Margaret was persuaded to stand in his place. She was extremely popular in the constituency; she was a magistrate, a member of Grimsby Education Committee and of Lincolnshire's agricultural committee. Even though the constituency was marginal, and she did not speak in public at all throughout the campaign as a mark of respect to her late husband, she was elected. She struck up an immediate friendship with Lady Astor; both were concerned over education, better milk supplies and temperance. In June 1922 Mrs Wintringham asked the Government to amend the Sex Disqualification (Removal) Act of 1919 to enable peeresses to sit in the House of Lords in their own right. This Act made it illegal to disqualify people on the grounds of their sex or marriage from exercising any public function. However, Viscountess Rhondda had been prevented from sitting in the Lords when the Lords' Committee of Privileges found that the Act simply removed disqualifications and did not confer rights that had not existed previously. Mrs Wintringham's attempt to remove this discrimination was rebuffed, and marked the start of a campaign that was to last until 1958, when women were finally allowed to sit in the Lords.

In 1921 the Women's Election Committee was founded to promote the cause of women candidates, and at the 1922 general election thirty-three women stood, almost double the number in 1918. This time there were sixteen Liberal candidates, ten Labour, five Conservatives and two Independents. Five of the Liberals had titles, and four of the Conservatives had titles or honours. The Labour candidates included Miss Margaret Bondfield and Miss Susan Lawrence; one of the Conservatives was Dame Helen Gwynne-Vaughan, professor of botany at London University and commander of the Women's Royal Air Force during the war. The two Independents were Miss Eleanor Rathbone, later to become a distinguished Parliamentarian, and Mrs Ray Strachey, who tried to become an M.P., and failed, at a number of subsequent elections.

In spite of the increase in the number of women who stood, all the women were defeated except Lady Astor and Mrs Wintringham – hardly surprising in view of the fact that most of them had been fighting what were thought of as unwinnable seats.

In 1923 a third woman crept into Westminster – yet another who inherited the seat from her husband. Mrs Mabel Hilton Philipson was well-known to the public as a musical comedy actress. Her husband, Captain Hilton Philipson, had been unseated in April 1923 as the National Liberal M.P. for Berwick-on-Tweed because of the fraudulent practices of his agent. Although he had not known of these practices, he was banned from standing as an M.P. for seven years and it was proposed that his wife should replace him. She agreed, provided she could stand as a Conservative – even though she was only acting as a 'warming-pan' for her husband's eventual return. She was elected, prompting Mrs Wintringham to remark to the *Daily Telegraph* on 8 June 1923: 'It is not a case of whether a woman is of my party or not. It is a case of whether she is going to help in our work, particularly in women's and children's questions and then, of course, the question of peace.'

The number of women M.P.s increased from three to eight at the 1923 general election – not because attitudes had suddenly changed, but because of the electoral swing, a factor that has directly affected the number of women elected ever since 1918. Thirty-four women stood, of whom twelve had stood before. Three Conservatives were elected, three Labour and two Liberals, and of the five new members, four won seats on their own account instead of inheriting them from their husbands. At last women M.P.s were beginning to reflect the concept of equality, of political activity in their own right, for which they had fought. Lady Terrington, wife of Baron Terrington, won Wycombe for the Liberals, ousting the sitting Conservative M.P. from a seat held almost continuously by his party since 1886. The three Labour women were the first unmarried women to be elected and the first women with careers, since they had all worked in the women's trade union movement. Susan Lawrence was returned in East Ham North, the daughter of a solicitor. She had read maths at Newnham College, Cambridge, and had been a Conservative until she found out how poorly charwomen were paid by the London County Council, resigned her seat on the L.C.C. and joined the Labour Party. She had spent six weeks in Holloway prison in 1921 for her part as one of the Poplar Guardians who refused to collect the poor rate – an experience she turned to good use by writing a pamphlet on taxation during her incarceration. She listed her interests in *Who's Who* as 'parties, Tolstoy, rowdy meetings, mountaineering and reading Government Blue Books'. She was clearly a formidable sight in Parliament. Ellen Wilkinson, in her book *Peeps at Politicians* published in 1931, said of Miss Lawrence: 'Tall, cold, severe, plainly dressed, at first when she rose to speak the House prepared for the worst; then they glimpsed the real Susan, the woman of delicate humour, of a merciless wit, of a logic they had believed was only masculine, of a mind which drank in facts as some men drink whisky.'

Miss Dorothy Jewson, the second Labour woman, who came from a similar middle-class background to Susan Lawrence, was another Cambridge graduate who had been an active suffragette. The third Labour woman, however, Miss Margaret Bondfield, was a type of woman new to Westminster. The daughter of a lacemaker, she became a shop assistant at fourteen and rose through the Shop Assistants' Union to become its general secretary. At the time of her election, her third attempt to enter Parliament, she was chairman of the T.U.C. General Council.

The Duchess of Atholl, the new woman M.P. who had inherited her seat from her husband, was a remarkable woman, whose horizons were to be broadened dramatically by her Parliamentary career. She won Perth and Kinross for the Conservatives, a seat held by her husband until 1917; she was honoured for her life of 'good works', but had opposed women's suffrage. Lloyd George suggested to her that she should stand for Parliament, because he wanted to see more women in the House, and hearing that many Conservative M.P.s were still unhappy about the presence of women in the Commons the Duchess, notwithstanding her previous opposition to women's suffrage, felt it her duty to try to smooth matters over by getting to Westminster herself. Her book, *Working Partnership*, records the speech she made just after her election in which she said: 'I think we still have to make the House of Commons and the nation realise what women can contribute to the work of Parliament and to do this, it seems to me, we have to use many of the qualities we find needed in our domestic life. Forty years ago, the ideal wife was one who said "Amen" to her husband whenever he opened his mouth. Today that idea has been abandoned and we have instead an ideal of comradeship, of partnership in life's happiness and difficulties alike which we recognise as much better.' This right-wing Tory woman was to evolve gradually into a rebel against her party; in 1938 she resigned her seat and fought a by-election in the cause of Republican Spain. She lost her seat by this stand against Fascism, and was reviled as a Communist by people who referred to her as 'The Red Duchess' – an extraordinary label for a woman of her background and earlier political persuasion.

In 1923, however, all this was still far in the future. In the meantime, Margaret Bondfield had inched forward the cause of women by being appointed Under-Secretary of State at the Ministry of Labour. Her maiden speech on unemployment had been regarded as the first intellectual speech to be delivered by a woman in the Commons. A few weeks later, in February 1924, Susan Lawrence was appointed Parliamentary Private Secretary to Mr Charles Trevelyan, President of the Board of Education. For her part, Dorothy Jewson used her maiden speech to second an attempt to amend the law to give women the vote at twenty-one, an attempt which was to fail. The Duchess of Atholl tried to block the motion, saying that the average housewife and mother did not want the vote since mothers with large families had no time for political meetings.

The 1924 general election saw a swing to the Conservatives and a reversal of women's fortunes. The three Conservative women, Lady Astor, the Duchess of Atholl and Mrs Hilton Philipson, were returned with increased majorities and one new Labour woman, Miss Ellen Wilkinson, was elected but all the others lost their seats. Labour had put up twenty-two women, the Conservatives twelve, the Liberals six, and there was one Independent, making a total of forty-one. Miss Wilkinson, daughter of a cotton worker turned insurance agent, had been educated at Manchester University and was known as 'Red Ellen' and 'The Fiery Particle' because of her left-wing views. A journalist and a trade union organiser, her goals were to secure equal rights for all classes of women and to improve the lives of all workers by inaugurating a socialist system. In 1925, during a debate on a Bill to bring Britain back on to the gold standard, she warned of the widespread unemployment that would follow – an unusual intervention by a woman in an economic debate. She introduced Bills to enable more women to join the police and to tighten up factory regulations to prevent industrial accidents, although neither measure reached the Statute Book.

During this Parliament, the number of women M.P.s was swelled by by-election victories. Susan Lawrence returned after the Conservative M.P. for East Ham North died, and made her reputation in Parliament during debates on the Local Government Bill and the Rating and Valuation Bills in 1928, impressing the House by her closely reasoned arguments and mastery of the facts. Margaret Bondfield returned to the Commons in 1926, and spoke mainly on unemployment. And in November 1927, the Countess of Iveagh inherited her husband's seat at Southend after he had succeeded to an earldom, emphasising the Conservative Party's reluctance to select women who had no marital claim to a seat. In the last eighteen months of the Parliament, three more women became M.P.s, swelling the total to ten. Two of them, Mrs Hilda Runciman and Mrs Ruth Dalton, joined their husbands Walter and Hugh in the House – but they were merely performing the function of keeping more attractive seats 'warm' for their husbands. The third woman was Miss Jennie Lee, daughter of a Fifeshire miner and at twenty-four then the youngest woman ever to have become an M.P.

Her election caused a huge sensation because of the irony of her age. For women were still not permitted to vote until they were thirty, an anomaly that was finally removed in March 1928 when Parliament at last agreed to give women the vote on the same terms as men. Pamela Brookes, in *Women at Westminster*, records that this came about because Lady Astor and Ellen Wilkinson had pushed the Home Secretary, Sir William Joynson-Hicks, into promising more than the Government had agreed. *Hansard* for 20 February 1925 shows that Sir William undertook not only that there would be no difference in the voting ages of men and women at the next election, but that it would be difficult to raise the voting age for men. But Mr Baldwin and his colleagues had actually been considering making the voting age for both sexes twenty-five. Mr Baldwin realised that Sir William's statement would have to be honoured and persuaded the Cabinet to agree. So the battle for the woman's franchise was finally won, ten years after the first woman had been elected to Parliament.

By the time of the 'Flapper election' of 1929, thirteen women had become M.P.s, seven of them in place of their husbands. In 1929, there were sixty-nine women candidates: thirty Labour, twenty-five Liberals, ten Conservatives and four others. Labour won the election, although not by an absolute majority, and fourteen women were elected; all the former women M.P.s except Mrs Runciman were returned. The new Labour women were Dr Ethel Bentham, Dr Marion Phillips, Mrs Mary Agnes Hamilton, Miss Edith Picton-Turbervill and Lady Cynthia Mosley. Miss Megan Lloyd George retained Anglesey for the Liberals,

THELMA CAZALET canvassing a maid in Islington East in October
1931. She successfully fought an all-woman contest against the Labour
candidate Mrs Leah Manning

Dr EDITH SUMMERSKILL speaking on freedom of the press at a meeting of the National Council for Civil Liberties in 1942

BARBARA WOOTTON, who was to become one of the first four women life Peers, at a meeting in Central Hall, London. Her husband said he wanted to become the first male Peeress and sit in the special gallery reserved for the spouses of Peers. He was stymied by the absence of a gentlemen's lavatory

A stereotype is perpetuated. This appeared in the *Punch Almanack* for 1853

THE PARLIAMENTARY FEMALE.

Father of the Family. "COME, DEAR; WE SO SELDOM GO OUT TOGETHER NOW—CAN'T YOU TAKE US ALL TO THE PLAY TO-NIGHT?"

Mistress of the House, and M.P. "HOW YOU TALK, CHARLES! DON'T YOU SEE THAT I AM TOO BUSY. I HAVE A COMMITTEE TO-MORROW RNING, AND I HAVE MY SPEECH ON THE GREAT CROCHET QUESTION TO PREPARE FOR THE EVENING."

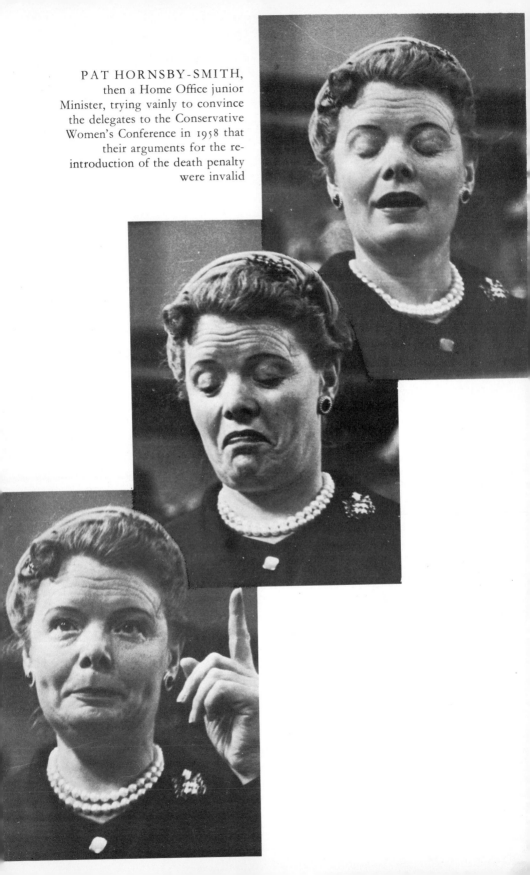

PAT HORNSBY-SMITH, then a Home Office junior Minister, trying vainly to convince the delegates to the Conservative Women's Conference in 1958 that their arguments for the re-introduction of the death penalty were invalid

and Miss Eleanor Rathbone who was returned for the Combined English Universities became the first Independent woman M.P. All these women, with the exception of Megan Lloyd George and Lady Mosley, whose husband Sir Oswald was Labour M.P. for Smethwick, won their seats without a shadow of family influence. Dr Bentham had pioneered a baby clinic; Miss Hamilton had taken a First in economics at Cambridge and was a journalist and pacifist intellectual; Miss Picton-Turbervill had been active in social work and, like Miss Hamilton, was a friend of Ramsay MacDonald; and Dr Phillips was the Chief Woman Officer of the Labour Party and one of the first women J.P.s. Miss Rathbone, however, was to make the most impact upon Parliament. Daughter of a former Liberal M.P., she had read Greats at Oxford; she had been a member of Liverpool City Council and president of the National Union of Societies for Equal Citizenship. A formidable blue-stocking, she was more admired than loved in the House as she battled for her two main causes: family allowances and the improvement of the position of Indian women.

Meanwhile, Margaret Bondfield had been appointed to a Cabinet post as Minister of Labour. It was a notable achievement, although a double-edged one. Her job was really to administer unemployment relief; dealing with the problem of unemployment itself was the job of a separate committee. She soon found herself pinioned at the Dispatch Box between an onslaught of criticism from the right, who thought that too much was being done for the unemployed, and from the left, who thought that not enough was being done. Miss Bondfield was the unfortunate pioneer of a trend that dogs women politicians to this day – the trend that puts able women into ministries which never have enough money to meet demand for the public services they provide, and consequently prove to be deadly political traps for the women appointed to run them. Margaret Bondfield at Labour, Ellen Wilkinson at the Ministry of Pensions, Edith Summerskill at the Ministry of Food, Mrs Thatcher at the Department of Education and Mrs Williams at the Prices Ministry all had to tread perilous political paths because of this.

The formation of a National Government in August 1931 brought the term of office of the first woman Cabinet Minister to an abrupt end. The ensuing general election also brought to an end the Parliamentary career of Susan Lawrence, who had been Parliamentary Secretary to the Ministry of Health and who was not to return to the Commons. The 1931 election saw sixty-two women candidates, seven fewer than in

1929. There were thirty-six Labour women, sixteen Conservatives, six Liberals and four others. There were two all-women fights: Mrs Leah Manning *v.* Miss Thelma Cazalet at Islington East, and Miss Bondfield *v.* Miss Irene Ward at Wallsend. The Labour Party was massacred at the election and returned no women. All the titled Conservative women – Lady Astor, the Duchess of Atholl and the Countess of Iveagh – were returned with increased majorities. There were also ten new Conservative women, one Liberal and one Independent, Miss Rathbone. Most of the new women had a background in voluntary social work and were not as notable as their predecessors. Two had had professional careers: Miss Marjorie Graves, who won Hackney South, had been employed in the Home Office Intelligence department after the war and was a member of Holborn Borough Council. And Miss Mary Pickford, daughter of the Master of the Rolls Lord Sterndale, had been technical adviser to the Government delegation to the International Labour Conference at Geneva.

At the 1935 general election, nine women were elected out of thirty-five Labour candidates, nineteen Conservatives, eleven Liberals and two others. Ellen Wilkinson was returned for Jarrow as the one Labour woman M.P. In the four years in which she had been absent from Westminster, she had written three books, visited India, the United States and Europe, and spoken at the last free election in Germany before the rise of Hitler. Foreign affairs and the threat of war overshadowed this Parliament, and Ellen Wilkinson and the Duchess of Atholl made strange bedfellows in their denunciations of Fascism. Women were active on domestic issues as well: on 1 April 1936 most of the women combined to defeat the Government by eight votes in support of Ellen Wilkinson's amendment aimed at providing equal pay for women in the civil service. The Duchess of Atholl, still an anti-feminist, was the only woman to vote with the Government. Ellen Wilkinson also agitated on behalf of the unemployed of Jarrow; Irene Ward introduced a Bill to enable old people in poor law institutions to receive pocket money; and Florence Horsbrugh introduced the Adoption of Children (Regulation) Bill. In June 1938 Miss Thelma Cazalet was appointed P.P.S. to Mr Kenneth Lindsay, Parliamentary Secretary at the Board of Education, and Miss Florence Horsbrugh was appointed Parliamentary Secretary to the Ministry of Health. By the end of 1938 there were twelve women M.P.s; although the Duchess of Atholl had lost her seat four women had been returned at by-elections, including Dr

Edith Summerskill.

It was during the Second World War that the women in Parliament came nearest to acting concertedly as a women's party. Another irony had emerged: whereas the First World War had helped create the climate of popular opinion that helped women to win the vote, the Second World War revealed an official reluctance to use women to any great extent, a reluctance that provoked the formation of a women's front in Parliament. Various women's organisations complained to the women M.P.s about the paltry number of women who had been offered war work. Although two women M.P.s had Government posts, in February 1940 the women Backbenchers lobbied the Financial Secretary to the Treasury to demand that women be given a more responsible role to play in the war effort. A committee of Backbenchers and other prominent women outside Parliament met fortnightly to monitor the position; in September 1941 it organised a deputation to the Foreign Secretary, Anthony Eden, to ask him to lift the ban on women entering the diplomatic and consular services. Another deputation went to see the Chancellor of the Exchequer to ask him to lift the marriage ban on women in the civil service. In 1941 and 1942, the women M.P.s forced two debates on woman-power which dealt with the whole range of grievances such as the shortage of day nurseries and the inadequate wages and conditions of women workers. *Hansard* records that on 20 March 1941 Mrs Thelma Cazalet-Keir said: 'If we had forty or fifty women Members of Parliament instead of the present small number I doubt whether this debate would have been necessary because many of the things we are discussing today would either never have occurred or would have been automatically rectified at a much earlier date . . . I'm sure that one of the tests of the civilisation of a country – and by civilisation I mean democratic way of life – is the position and status given to women.'

One particular grievance was that women received less compensation than men for their war injuries. Mrs Mavis Tate forced a division on the issue, and as a result a select committee was set up which eventually abolished the discrimination. Dr Summerskill objected strongly to a propaganda poster which advised: 'Be Like Dad, Keep Mum.' And in 1944 Mrs Cazalet-Keir moved an amendment to give equal pay to women teachers. All this activity on behalf of women was taking place under a Prime Minister, Mr Winston Churchill, who had never supported the women's cause. Several years later, in 1951, he was to make Florence Horsbrugh Minister of Education but without a seat in the Cabinet – the first time an Education Minister had been excluded from the Cabinet for twenty years. In 1944, he reacted strongly to Mrs Cazalet-Keir's Bill for equal pay for teachers, and made a vote to delete the offending clause a vote of confidence. The clause was lost, and the cause of equal pay put back once again.

The 1945 general election provided women with their greatest Parliamentary triumph and seemed to indicate that at last women were making significant inroads into Westminster. Out of 1,683 candidates, eighty-seven were women; Labour won a landslide majority and twenty-four women were elected, among them twenty-one Labour, one Conservative, one Liberal and one Independent. A large number of these new women were teachers, and several described themselves as 'house-wives'. Eleven of the twelve new Labour members had won Conservative-held seats; the three youngest Members were in their thirties and had got into Parliament at their first attempt: Miss Alice Bacon, Miss Margaret Herbison and Mrs Barbara Castle. Most of the women had records of public service, and again were less impressive than the very early pioneers. Mrs Barbara Ayrton Gould, who had fought every general election since 1922, had been a militant suffragette and was one of the few in the 1945 Parliament who had direct links with that period. The Prime Minister, Mr Clement Attlee, made Ellen Wilkinson Minister of Education and Dr Summerskill Parliamentary Secretary to the Ministry of Food, where she piloted through legislation making the pasteurisation of milk compulsory. Jennie Adamson became Parliamentary Secretary to the Ministry of Pensions; Barbara Castle was appointed P.P.S. to Sir Stafford Cripps, President of the Board of Trade; and Jennie Lee went to the Central Advisory Committee on Housing.

Any idea that the 1945 result was a breakthrough for women was soon scotched, however. In 1950, only twenty-one women were returned in an election which reduced Labour's majority to six seats; this underlined the sad fact that the success of women candidates depended greatly on a swing towards Labour. This was because the Labour Party consistently selected women for marginal or even apparently hopeless seats – and the Labour Party selected more women than did the Conservatives. The Conservative women candidates actually stood more chance of being elected although there were fewer of them. Throughout the postwar years, the number of women elected to Parliament has never risen above the twenty-nine returned at the 1964 general election.

The last major constitutional battle to be fought on behalf of women was won in 1958 when, despite vociferous opposition, women became able to take their place in the House of Lords as peers on an equal basis to men. Several citadels remain to be stormed: no woman has ever become Chancellor of the Exchequer or Attorney-General, posts which remain entrenched male domains. Nevertheless the most disappointing memorial to the early suffragists and the formidable women who pioneered the women's cause in Parliament remains the derisory number of women M.P.s. Until the barriers at local level are broken down, and women are selected in large numbers for seats that can be won without benefit of a swing of landslide proportions, women will continue to be conspicuous in Parliament as oddities; the successors to Margaret Bondfield and Eleanor Rathbone will continue to be no more than symbolic representatives of a lost cause.

3 *The Road to Parliament*

THE most extraordinary thing about the women who are at present members of the House of Commons is that they appear to be so very ordinary. They are worthy ladies, easier to imagine as schoolteachers, magistrates or local councillors – as, indeed, many of them have been – than as members of the tiny élite of women who have made it in national politics. Because there are so few of them, one expects them to possess exceptional characteristics, even to the point of eccentricity. One expects presence, charisma, a certain showmanship. Such attributes are noticeable among some of the older women who have now left the Commons. Lady Summerskill, who gained a reputation in Parliament as a formidable campaigner for women's rights, was still, when I saw her, a stern, uncompromising, forbidding figure. Lady Vickers, who as Conservative M.P. for Plymouth held on to her unlikely working-class constituency through the loyalty and devotion of her constituents, stands out from the Parliamentary throng in her distinctive apparel of elegant veil and choker of pearls. Even Barbara Castle, who retired from the Commons at the 1979 general election and so does not yet command the respect that often accompanies nostalgia, possesses an aura of personal magnetism that causes heads to turn in her direction. She personifies qualities one might expect from all these rare women M.P.s; a gift of oratory, an outstanding intellect, a passionate commitment to a cause. But many of the other women M.P.s to whom I spoke were diffident, even shy; nor were they fine public speakers. The intelligence of most of them shone out like a beacon, but only by way of illuminating the dull stupidity of many of their male colleagues. The women M.P.s appeared to be no more able intellectually than many of the women who have reached the top in other professions. And as for passionate commitment, most of them had apparently been nudged into Parliament by a combination of luck and whim.

But they are, of course, far from ordinary. Although most could easily fit into the categories of schoolteachers, secretaries, businesswomen or lawyers, few women in these careers could slip as easily into the role of a Member of Parliament. There is no doubt that for a woman the path to Westminster is strewn with far more obstacles than beset a man, and the women who get there must have certain qualities to enable them to stay the course. Any idea that Mrs Thatcher's rise to power will open the floodgates to the proportional representation of women at Westminster must be scotched. The factors which gave her victory were a unique combination, and few women are going to be able to relate the particulars of Mrs Thatcher's own personality, circumstances and career to their own lives. One senior regional Conservative Party worker told me that, after Mrs Thatcher was elected leader of the party in 1975, there was actually increased hostility among the constituency parties towards the idea of selecting women candidates. The main reason for this hostility seemed to be that the Parliamentary Backbenchers who had elected Mrs Thatcher were out of tune with feeling in many of the constituencies. These were still loyal to Edward Heath, and fiercely resented the person who had deposed him. This resentment expressed itself in a hostile attitude towards people of the same sex as the 'upstart' new leader, women who had the audacity to want to follow Mrs Thatcher into public life. That resentment has now obviously been dissipated, but there are still no signs that Mrs Thatcher's success will substantially raise the number of women M.P.s.

Few women are going to be able to push aside the barriers that still exist, both in their own minds and in the community – barriers of prejudice and hostility created by traditional assumptions about the role that women should play in society. These assumptions have now been questioned, but any movement away from them is painfully slow. The progress that has been made in the attempt to achieve equal rights for women has merely tinkered on the fringes of these entrenched attitudes, although the publicity that has accompanied these manoeuvres seems to have persuaded many people that full equality of opportunity has already arrived – and may even be a bad thing. Those who are bored by the subject are happy to push it into the bureaucratic queue, to make women take their place among all the other troublesome disadvantaged groups clamouring for equal rights. After all, the subject of women's rights has now been codified into laws like the Sex Discrimination Act and the Equal Pay Act and it has its very own quango, the Equal Opportunities Commission, to look after it. What more, ask the exasperated reactionaries, can women possibly want?

But the provisions of the Equal Pay Act can be, and all too easily are, circumnavigated. The Sex Discrimination Act becomes toothless in the absence of practical measures such as widespread creche or nursery provision. As for the Equal Opportunities Commission, the *Guardian* has aptly characterised it as 'a rather wet, ladylike body too concerned with holding its skirts down against the rude winds to have a go at entrenched masculine strongholds'. Furthermore, since Mrs Thatcher's Government took office, there have been clear indications that the limited advances that have been made towards equal opportunities for women are now under attack. Maternity leave provisions, which enable women to return to work after having babies, have been threatened. Mr Patrick Jenkin, Social Services Secretary, has delivered himself of the opinion that more women should stay at home and look after their children rather than go out to work. Enforced separation of children from their mothers during the last war, he announced, was responsible for many current social ills. State day nurseries, and other childminding provisions, should only be provided for the most disadvantaged.

The message could not be clearer. As structural unemployment tightens its grip on Britain, women are again becoming regarded as expendable workers who should return to their rightful place in the home. The fact that many ordinary women now have to work to maintain their families seems to be disregarded by the woman who is presiding over these policies and turning back the clock of emancipation.

Meanwhile, social attitudes have remained largely unchanged despite the political advances that have occurred. At school, at home, through the advertising that bombards them, girls are made to feel that domesticity should be the cornerstone of their lives. At school they still shy away from 'masculine' subjects like science and economics. Women often hide considerable abilities behind a mask of diffidence or shyness.

If they go to public meetings, they tend to be silent. Several M.P.s told me of meetings they had addressed after which there would be no question asked by a woman; but after the proceedings had finished, a woman would approach them quietly and ask a question that was far more perceptive than those that had been asked in public. It is as if they are frightened that they will be laughed at if they commit themselves in public; they do not think of themselves as public performers. It may also be that those who do push themselves on to a public platform do so with a purpose in mind: they want to become secretary of their union branch, for example, or they hope to be spotted at party conferences by political talent scouts. Women are less likely to be driven by long-term ambitions of this kind. They do not see themselves as the union branch secretary or the M.P., because for them the stereotyped image in which they were moulded has been translated into practical reality.

For even if they work – and today many women work not for pin money but because their families need their wages – they are still expected to undertake the same domestic responsibilities as if they did not. They have to cook and clean and wash and iron; they have to think about what the family is going to eat and shop accordingly; they have to take time off work to nurse sick children. Their menfolk still assume, by and large, that they do not have to do these things. Again, this is changing slowly, particularly among young people, but in the main the woman who works undertakes two full-time jobs. Even those who would once have been wealthy enough to employ servants, in the days when servants were an accepted part of affluent households, can no longer automatically assume that they will be able to employ nannies, cooks and maids.

These domestic commitments mean that, for the vast majority of women, public life cannot even be considered. And there are other powerful deterrents for a woman who has any desire to become an M.P. For a start, it costs money. If a woman lives in Yorkshire, and is selected to fight a seat in Devon, it will cost her a small fortune in fares and accommodation if she is to nurse the seat conscientiously over a number of years. Relatively few women are employed in professions which not only pay well enough to enable them to do this, but also provide sufficiently flexible working arrangements. And women notoriously are selected mainly for marginal seats, which means that they will be forced to repeat this process again and again.

But their predicament is often not improved even if they do stand a good chance of winning the seat, since if they win they will have to move up to London, at least for a good part of every week while the Parliamentary session is in progress. Yet they may have husbands or families who do not wish to move or who cannot do so for a number of reasons. The logistic problems are by no means as severe for the new male M.P., since he will expect his wife to move to wherever he has to be based, and normally she will accept this as part of her role. And for those women who already live in London or in areas easily accessible to Westminster, the anti-social hours that Parliament sits, often until the early hours of the morning, make the prospect of becoming an M.P. extremely unattractive.

So why do they do it? Are there common factors in the backgrounds and characters of women M.P.s which enable one to trace some kind of pattern that links them all? One of the most surprising points about them is that so few were driven to stand for Parliament by long-standing, urgent ambition. In view of all the difficulties in their way, one might have thought that most would always have nourished a desire to become M.P.s. But in fact only a very few said that this had been the case. For the majority, chance had played a large part – although once started on the Parliamentary trail, they all seemed to succumb to the mysteriously forceful pull of political life.

One might also assume that the fact that many of them came from political backgrounds made it somehow inevitable that they would end up in Parliament. This, too, would be a false generalisation. The political families from which some of them came were obviously important in shaping their political consciousness and familiarising them with the language, customs and personalities of politics. Nevertheless, the women M.P.s often had brothers and sisters whose interest in politics didn't match their own. Shirley Summerskill, for instance, daughter of the former Labour Minister Dr Edith Summerskill, points to her brother as proof that it was not at all inevitable that she should have followed her mother to Westminster. Her brother was, it is true, chairman of the Labour club at Oxford where Shirley was treasurer, but he lost his interest in politics after he became a barrister. Their childhood was dominated by elections and by-elections and political discussion, and the house was always full of political visitors. Both Edith Summerskill and her husband, Jeffrey Samuel, were doctors, and it was in the family tradition of medicine that Shirley felt it was almost inevitable she should have followed. 'I don't feel that I'm a replica of my mother, nor did I want to be; I just wanted to be a doctor,' she told me. 'Medicine sustained my political interest, because medical practice is rather like being an M.P., with surgeries and so on.'

In some cases, the political experiences of their fathers provided a disincentive to their daughters to enter Parliament. Gwyneth Dunwoody knew from her father's involvement what strains a political life imposes. Her father was Morgan Phillips, a General Secretary of the Labour Party, and Mrs Dunwoody, who entered Parliament in 1966, feels that she was virtually brought up in the Palace of Westminster. 'My father wouldn't have wanted me to go into politics,' she told me. 'It's not an easy life and claims a fairly high price – he knew that better than anyone as he suffered a stroke. I certainly wouldn't encourage my children to go into it.'

Despite her reluctance, Mrs Dunwoody was drawn into the political arena. She became a local councillor in Totnes simply to frustrate the local Conservative candidate who would otherwise have been returned unopposed, and was persuaded to stand for Exeter by the women of the local party, who were tired of male candidates. Mrs Dunwoody, who cheerfully admits to being lazy, didn't want the bother of fighting an election, although she enjoyed it in the end and went on to become the member for Crewe. 'It's always been women who have supported me,' she said. 'They used to zip me into evening dresses and push me into trains. I didn't want the work; you've really got to work at a constituency, get to know the local activists, and it's quite hard. But once I had done it and found I was quite good at it – that was quite different.'

Eirene White, now Baroness White, who was a Labour Minister during the 1960s, reacted not so much against the grind of Parliamentary politics as against their moral squalor. Her father, Dr Thomas Jones, who had been a deputy secretary to the Cabinet during the First World War, had become deeply disillusioned by the Labour politicians he had served. He was a former professor of political economy, and Lady White's mother was a Cambridge graduate who was active in the Co-operative movement, so it was perhaps inevitable that when Lady White came down from Oxford in the 1930s she should develop a keen political awareness. At Oxford, one of her closest friends was Sheila MacDonald, youngest daughter of the first Labour Prime Minister Ramsay MacDonald. Relations between MacDonald and Dr Jones were not, however, very cordial, and her father's experiences imbued Lady

White with a certain prejudice against politicians. 'In the first Labour government, Ramsay MacDonald was so suspicious of anyone who had been in Downing Street already that he wouldn't use my father at all,' she said. Then there was the Campbell affair. John Ross Campbell, an assistant editor of *Workers' Weekly*, was arrested on a charge of incitement to mutiny. The minutes of the relevant Cabinet meeting show that the Cabinet decided to drop the prosecution, although MacDonald then denied he had been consulted about the affair at all, a discrepancy that led Dr Jones to describe MacDonald's statement as 'a bloody lie'.

Despite her misgivings about politicians, Lady White decided to stand for Parliament in 1945. There were various reasons for her decision. She had gone to work at the Ministry of Labour, but since she had not taken the administrative examination there was little chance of promotion and a civil service career. So she was on the lookout for an alternative. 'Also, some of my generation realised that things had gone very badly indeed after the First War and one would hope to do something better after the Second, and I felt I would like to be much more involved than being a small cog in a departmental wheel would allow one to be,' she said. The matter was clinched after she attended a Fabian summer school where she was able to observe four men of indifferent quality who had been selected as Parliamentary candidates. 'At the end of the school, having heard them, I said to myself: if they can do it, I can as well,' she remembered.

One side-effect of a political background which has now disappeared was the relative ease with which women used to be able to take over their husbands' seats when they died or retired. Today, M.P.s' wives, particularly in the Conservative Party, are expected to undertake a certain amount of constituency work on their husbands' behalf, but inheriting the seat is another matter. Lady Davidson, who became M.P. for Hemel Hempstead after her husband retired from the seat in 1937, built up a considerable reputation for herself in this way. She had been brought up in a political family, since her father was the Liberal M.P. Sir Willoughby Dickinson, but she really only became interested in politics when she married in 1919. Her husband, Viscount Davidson, worked as a private secretary to Bonar Law, the Conservative Prime Minister. 'He was frightfully interested in the work he was doing in Downing Street, and I couldn't be anything but interested – I was brought up to be interested,' Lady Davidson told me. 'I got a little house near Parliament;

I knew enough of politics to know that otherwise I would never see my husband at all. I did a lot in the constituency; he was very tied up in London, and it was my job to do it. We had to be able to do it. We were all lucky enough to have nannies and nursemaids; today, of course, it's extremely difficult. I ran the constituency with a good agent. We worked from London, but I went to everything I could go to and they knew they could always call on me.' In view of the way she had stamped her personality on the constituency, it was hardly surprising that she should have been called upon when her husband retired. 'I was in the bath when the phone went and they asked me to stand,' she recalled. 'I was so astonished – but I was dripping wet and cold and so I said yes.'

This cosy nepotism has now disappeared, although it is still easier for women to become M.P.s if through their early backgrounds or careers they have made themselves known in the appropriate party circles. Even though a political upbringing does not point an automatic way to a Parliamentary career, there is no doubt that it is an important formative influence. It would have been difficult for some of the women who have entered Parliament not to have accepted politics as an integral part of their lives. Alice Bacon, now Baroness Bacon, joined the Labour Party as a matter of course, and the desire to stand for Parliament evolved as a natural progression. Born in 1911 and brought up in Yorkshire, she was the daughter of a miner and local trade union leader. Her mother was also involved in union work, and the house was a focal point for M.P.s and local party workers. Lady Bacon recalled that Herbert Morrison, later to become a Labour Home Secretary, was a frequent visitor and was extremely partial to her mother's home cooking. 'He went to America, where apparently he declared that the food wasn't as good as it was at Mrs Bacon's. The next thing was that a phone call came through from New York asking for one of my mother's recipes! My mother didn't turn a hair, but gave the recipe as coolly as anything'.

There is a striking difference, however, between the political involvement of the families of the Labour women and that of the Conservatives' families. Most of the Labour women now in the Commons have been steeped in politics since childhood, but the reverse is true among the Conservatives. On the Labour side, Jo Richardson, whose father stood unsuccessfully for Parliament during the 1930s, says she had politics rammed down her throat as a child. Joan Lestor describes herself as a 'cradle socialist': her father was a political organiser for the Canadian arm of the Socialist Party of Great Britain, and her mother was a shop steward of a garment workers' union, an unusual role for a woman to play in those days. Betty Boothroyd says she virtually grew up in the Labour Party as her father, a textile designer, and her mother, a weaver, were both ardent trade unionists. And Ann Taylor remembers as a child going round canvassing with her father who helped out for the local party in Bolton. Her own political interest, she told me, flowered out of a sense of isolation. Her father was a telephone engineer, and Ann was the only child at her direct grant school to live on a council estate. The feeling of 'being different' came to a head when she was thirteen. 'I was at this "snob factory" when there was a crucial by-election in Bolton in 1960. I was obviously in a very tiny minority of support for the Labour Party at school, and for some reason the whole thing took off for me at that point.'

Even if their parents weren't active in party politics, they often possessed strong moral or religious beliefs. Both Joyce Butler and Dame Judith Hart were deeply influenced by the moral preoccupations of their parents. Mrs Butler's Quaker parents were concerned about social issues and were strongly opposed to war, a position shared by their daughter. 'My main interest in socialism was that it seemed to me that if you had a completely socialist system, many of the trade crises would disappear,' she said. 'At school, I remember being very struck by Disraeli's book *Sybil*, which was a revelation to me. We were not well off, but we were not desperately badly off, and I remember being appalled by the desperation of the working-class women in *Sybil*. Everyone I knew then assumed that women didn't go out to work; here was the working class revealed.'

Moral issues figured prominently in Judith Hart's upbringing. Her father, a linotype operator, and her mother, who was a teacher and died when Dame Judith was fifteen, were active members of the Progressive Baptist Church in Lancashire. Her father was the choirmaster there, and her mother was a lay preacher, a pacifist who took up causes such as prejudice against unmarried mothers. In her teens, the young Judith decided she wanted to find out more about the system that was producing the mass unemployment that surrounded her in Lancashire during the 1930s, so she borrowed the first volume of *Das Kapital* from Burnley public library. She recalls, wryly, that she made little progress with it. But by the time she was fifteen she was known at school as a committed socialist.

The Conservative women, on the other hand, were mostly not

brought up in such a ferment of political activity. A couple came from families where some Parliamentary ambition had been nourished. Janet Fookes's grandfather had wanted to be an M.P. and her parents were interested in politics; and Lynda Chalker remembers vividly her father's disappointment when he was beaten to the nomination for the Southend seat by four votes. 'I was sixteen at the time, and it was the first time I'd seen anyone beaten by political manoeuvring,' she recalled. Jill Knight's family were not interested in politics at all; Sally Oppenheim's parents were no more than staunch Conservative voters, as were Sheila Faith's; and Peggy Fenner virtually had no family at all. Brought up by her grandparents from the age of six months, she was sent to an L.C.C. school which she left when she was fourteen; she married when she was eighteen and had her first baby at nineteen – hardly, one might think, a conventional training ground for a Conservative M.P. Elaine Kellett-Bowman's father thought that politics was a dirty business. 'But he used to say, if you don't agree with how the game is played, then you should get into it,' she said.

His advice might well be a motto for many Conservative women. For, oddly enough, they tended to be far more highly motivated than the Labour women. Despite the high level of political or moral concern among their families, the Labour women were mainly drawn into national politics gradually and almost despite themselves. But a far larger proportion of Conservatives said they had fulfilled a childhood ambition when they were elected to Westminster, an ambition they had taken considerable pains to realise. Both Jill Knight and Elaine Kellett-Bowman said that their political ambitions had been shaped by similar experiences at school. 'I always wanted to get into Parliament and I knew I would,' Mrs Kellett-Bowman told me. 'I went to a grammar school which taught economics and politics very seriously. We had a current affairs teacher who was a very committed socialist, the daughter of a mine manager, who used to go on and on. Even to twelve and thirteen-year-olds, her views were so obviously unfair that a friend and I used to go into the library and read up things that made us become Tories.' At thirteen, Mrs Knight reacted in a similar fashion against her Fabian schoolteacher. 'She thought her duty was to indoctrinate all her charges, and the more she told me about socialism, the more I thought how bad it was and so I decided to go into Parliament,' she said. 'I thought socialism was such rubbish, and I cared very much about the country. Because I cared for it, and because of what had almost happened to it during the war, I wanted to make sure that when the war was over we had a sensible and good Government.'

Janet Fookes, who displayed considerable application in getting into Parliament, seems to have been driven by an almost mystical sense that she was destined to become an M.P. Her father was director of a confectionery firm and the family was comfortably off, but Miss Fookes believed that her political ambition was in some way inherited from her grandfather, who had actually supported the Labour Party. 'He had an idealistic sense of the needs of the working people, the idealistic approach of someone from the upper middle classes,' Miss Fookes said. 'He died before I was born, but my family say I am like him in many ways. I know I mentioned that I wanted to be an M.P. when I was interviewed by a board of governors for a scholarship when I was eleven. I probably felt it before that. I don't know how my imagination was fired in this way; it was just something that I felt very deeply and wanted to do. It seemed to be something inside me from the very beginning. My parents always allowed me to think for myself. I wanted to be an M.P. before I wanted to be a Conservative. There were times when it seemed very remote, almost impossible to turn it into practical reality.'

Two teachers at her junior school helped foster Janet's ambition. 'One encouraged us to speak in public. When we were seven or eight, she made us stand up and give speeches and then she would hold an inquest into the good points and the bad. Another teacher told us never to adopt the politics of our parents, but always to think for ourselves. They had great influence, but they were working on receptive soil.' At London University, she joined the Conservative Association and got on with the serious business of preparing herself for a Parliamentary career. In her first year, she took lessons in voice production, then she went on to take examinations in public speaking at the Guildhall School of Music and Drama. After her finals, she took a year off and helped out in her local party. 'The agent was a woman of some experience who was rather lugubrious and said I didn't stand a chance of a political career,' she recalled cheerfully.

Some of the women to whom I spoke felt that, at school or at university, they had had to battle against preconceptions about the role of women. Curiously, though, it was the younger women who complained most about this. Older women such as Lady Bacon had never felt their sex to be a disadvantage. The fact that she was a girl had never been considered significant in the mining community where she grew up, she told me. Putting herself forward as a Parliamentary candidate for her industrial Leeds constituency did not seem at all unusual. 'The fact that I was a woman never entered into it,' she said. 'I was always used to living among working-class men. Years ago, the working man's club was the focal point of community life. My mother used to go and make sandwiches for them, they used to take children to the seaside for the day, and I was always used to being in all this. My selection for the Leeds seat took place in a working men's club. The other candidate said afterwards that he had wanted to apologise for bringing me there, but he was the one who felt out of place, not me. It was nothing to do with being a man or a woman; it was a question of upbringing. But there are no longer any working-class young men or women M.P.s. They have lost touch with the working-class population, and in many ways it's a retrograde step that they are now all well-educated, middle-class M.P.s.'

Several younger women, however, complained that they had been made to feel freakish on account of their political interest, particularly those who went to public or direct grant schools. Politics was regarded as an activity to be pursued by men, not quite genteel even for girls who were being educated to go on to university and pursue a career. Shirley Summerskill had to battle against this kind of conditioning, even though her mother had enjoyed a distinguished Parliamentary career. Shirley Summerskill recalled: 'When I first expressed a desire to be an M.P. thirty years ago, the girls at school laughed and the teachers thought I was a bit odd. And yet I was in an exceptional position because of my mother; they all knew who she was.' Others did not have the psychological booster of a Parliamentary pioneer in the family. Ann Taylor decided in her early teens that she wanted a job in politics. She joined the Young Socialists and thought of becoming a party agent – never an M.P., since these were very special and peculiar people whom she had never met. She drifted into the sixth form at school, but discovered that it didn't teach economic history or politics, the subjects in which she was most interested. So while she continued her sixth-form studies, she enrolled at night school where she supplemented her school work with studies in British government. Only there was she told, to her delight, that it was possible to study politics at university, which she proceeded to do.

Many women M.P.s were helped into politics, or at least into their political awareness, by the feeling that they had been seen as different at school. Their isolation from their peers reinforced their attachment to the political background they had been given at home. But only Margaret Jackson, who lost her seat at the last election, actually was different and broke out of the arts graduate stereotype of Parliamentary women. She had seen grave hardship in her family. Her father, a carpenter, became an invalid when she was three years old and the family had to be supported on the earnings of her mother, who was a teacher. 'My mother was a Catholic with a very Christian approach of doing good for others and helping the poor,' she said. 'By the time I was in my teens I felt strongly that everyone had a duty to help in society and I was very conscious of the fact that we as a family had been damaged very severely by this tremendous stroke of bad luck. My sisters and I had all got scholarships and we could just afford the school uniforms. But it was a tremendous struggle; we lived on a knife edge. I thought about going into social work, but I thought politics was where the rules were made.'

She decided to become a metallurgist and took a sandwich course which combined college studies with work on the factory floor. 'I was at Manchester College of Science and Technology and at the freshers' dance, when people asked what I was studying, and I said metallurgy, they would say "What!" and I always got rather a kick out of that. I was absolutely determined not to be the sort of woman who has grey hair in a bun and wears lisle stockings. I fell over myself to wear perfume and dress reasonably well.'

For many M.P.s the decision to stand for Parliament evolved naturally out of their work in local government or in party organis- ations. Margaret Jackson, for example, was a research assistant at Transport House for four years, after which she became a special adviser to Judith Hart at the Ministry of Overseas Development, a career which provided a valuable political education. Judith Hart herself became involved in public life almost as a chore for the Labour Party. At London University she had been involved in the Labour club, but when she came down she married and became a sociology lecturer. 'I was going to be a good professional sociologist,' she remembered somewhat wryly. 'One was engaged in doing professional work and local party and union affairs, just as one does. There wasn't the slightest idea of going into Parliament. One thought of M.P.s as being aged about sixty or seventy, and I had no ambitions there at all. I just did research.'

But when she was twenty-five, the party asked her to stand as a municipal candidate at Parkstone in Dorset, near where she lived. It was a hopeless seat and consequently Dame Judith found it all tremendous fun. As a local candidate with a young baby, she generated quite a bit of excitement; she achieved a huge turnout and a low Tory majority. In 1950, she chaired some election meetings, including one where she had to speak off-the-cuff for an hour because Herbert Morrison, the major attraction, had been delayed elsewhere. The following year, she was drawn in deeper when she was asked to fight Bournemouth West, a seat which commanded one of the highest Conservative majorities in the country. She agreed to do so, even though before the election the family moved to Scotland, where her husband had just been appointed a university lecturer. Dame Judith knew that the resulting upheaval would only last for the duration of the election itself, since she stood no chance of winning the seat. So she moved down to Bournemouth for the campaign, complete with her child and its grandmother.

After that, she devoted herself to bringing up her children in Scotland. 'I was very much committed to bringing up my two children myself while they were small, because of the psychological side; I didn't trust anybody except myself,' she said. 'I was clear in my mind that they were going to have me, not a substitute mother. I was writing a little and doing adult education lecturing in the evening, all the things women in that position do to keep themselves going.' However, the party determined to enlist her talents, and after she fought another hopeless seat as a chore for the party, this time in Scotland, the almost inevitable dilemma finally arrived when she was asked to stand for the marginal constituency of Lanark. It was a traumatic decision to take. 'It meant asking myself whether I minded giving up university work and taking the risk of getting elected to Parliament. What decided it for me, because it took a lot of thinking about, was that since my professional interest was sociology, and the interests and welfare of people, that led to the question of where the power really lay – was it with a university researcher, or did it lie at Westminster? On that basis I decided, in a family decision, that I would go forward to the selection conference.'

Local government, however, remains the most popular route into Parliament. Some women used it deliberately as a training ground for their Parliamentary ambition; others found themselves propelled into a Parliamentary nomination as a result of their work on local councils, which provided an effective platform for displaying their talents. Some men, indeed, thought that local government should be the limit of

public life for women. Lady Vickers recalled receiving little encouragement for her Parliamentary ambitions from Winston Churchill, whose
brother happened to be her guardian. 'I was having lunch with Winston
one day,' she told me, 'and he asked me what I was going to do in life. I
said that I wanted to follow in his footsteps, to which he replied that
there should be no women in Parliament! He suggested that I should go
on to the L.C.C. instead. "Wear a pretty hat," he said, "and sit there and
you will get your own way." I thought that was quite a good idea,
because I knew there was quite a good chance of getting on to it at that
time.'

Despite such idiosyncratic dismissiveness, many women have found
in local government a way of combining a political life with domestic
commitments. Some, like Jill Knight and Janet Fookes, who had set
their sights on Parliament, deliberately used local government as a
training ground. Jill Knight was single-minded about it: 'I knew that if I
was going to get married and have children, I'd better get that over with
quickly, so I did. Then I thought the best thing was to get trained to get
into Parliament. So I got on to Northampton Council. This worked in
very well with babysitting and when the children were at school. I used
to rush back home and get them their tea.'

Peggy Fenner and Baroness Pike were two women who went into
local government with no thought of a Parliamentary career. Mrs
Fenner never thought of standing for Parliament, she said, because she
assumed that only highly educated women were accepted as candidates.
Not only had she left school at fourteen, but her rough youth had not
lent itself to political thought. But after she married, she decided to
attend the monthly council meetings to hear the reasons for the decisions
being taken. Every month, she was conspicuous as the solitary person in
the public gallery. Her house was also conspicuous on the solid Labour
council estate where she lived, since it was the only one to sport a
Conservative poster at election time. When a Tory council candidate
suddenly announced he was going to stand as an Independent at a council
election, the party asked Mrs Fenner to stand in his place – simply, she
said, because she had been noticed in this way.

Local politics were, until the end of the 1950s, far less polarised along
party lines than they are today, and they were able to accommodate with
greater ease changes in political allegiance. Lady Pike, whose family ran
an international mining business, became a socialist during the war, a
brief political flirtation which she now explains away as a temporary

aberration. 'It was almost an unexpressed criticism of the management of affairs between the wars. I thought that perhaps we hadn't changed the social structure fast enough. I was very keen on things like the National Health Service, and felt at the time that there was a better prospect of these things happening under the socialists. I changed to Conservatism because I am against nationalisation and central controls and I began to see, about 1950, that the system wasn't working. Also, I don't like envy, and from a philosophical point of view I think it was the realisation that envy seemed to be one of the motivating forces of socialism.'

This change in her politics didn't make much difference to her activities in local government, into which she drifted after the war. Her father had been a member of the local council, and her mother had belonged to almost everything else, so it was not surprising that she should have become involved in public life. The manner in which she got on to the local council, however, provides a charming reminder of the days when local politics were just that. The postman was chairman of the local Labour Party, and just after Lady Pike was demobbed he approached her. 'He came along and said, we think you'd better be chairman of the parish council,' she remembered. 'Then later, when I began to fall out with him, he said, we'd better get you on to the rural. I was very lucky because I was unopposed. In those days, this wasn't unusual if they felt they had someone good. I went on to the rural district council as a Conservative, but they thought I was independent-minded and so were happy not to oppose me. There wasn't then this awful polarisation that there is today. We were all of a generation; some were Conservative and some were Labour but it didn't matter that much. We didn't have whips; we voted how we thought.' The future Government Minister entertained no Parliamentary ambition until 1951 when Lord Walton, the Conservative Party chairman, suggested she might fight an election. 'My first reaction was that I wouldn't like the life in Parliament,' she said. 'I didn't particularly want to come and live in London; I never thought the levers of power were there. But it was the opportunity to express my views publicly that encouraged me.'

Fewer women now regard local government as the best stepping stone to Parliament than they did twenty years ago, a fact which has grieved Joyce Butler. Elected at Wood Green in 1955, she retired at the general election of 1979 and was replaced by a male candidate. She was chosen originally because she was well known to the selection committee, having lived in the constituency and been leader of the

Labour group on the council. A degree of luck was also involved; the sitting Labour member for the constituency had left it to the last minute before the election to announce that he wouldn't be standing again, so very few candidates had applied for this plum seat. Mrs Butler benefited because her name was well known and she was on the spot. When she announced her retirement, she was anxious that a woman should succeed her as Labour candidate, since she was aware that through her retirement the already tiny number of women M.P.s would be depleted still further. But among the large number of candidates who presented themselves for selection at Wood Green, none was involved in the council election which was taking place at the same time. So at a stroke one of the biggest advantages offered by women to many selection committees – that they are well known through their work on the council – was removed. 'This was a big disadvantage,' said Mrs Butler. 'If you've got a long list of candidates, it's simplest to cut it down by cutting out all the women and leaving only one woman on it. And women who have limited time cannot be in all the places where influence counts. I wrote to various women councillors afterwards asking them why they had not put their names forward, but I got no reply.' It was a disappointing end to a career which seemed to have fizzled out. 'I feel that a lot of the steam has gone out of me and out of Parliament and the political scene generally,' she told me before the general election. 'There are now so many able young people in the House, and I would have hated to carry on until people said, get out.'

Local government provides women with an opportunity to make their political name and to forge important friendships. For it is one thing to aspire to Parliament and quite another to translate that aspiration into practice. Year after year, both Labour and Conservative Parties express the pious hope that more women will present themselves for selection, that more constituencies will adopt women and that more women will be elected to Parliament. There seems to be something of a gap, however, between the exhortations of Transport House and Central Office and the realities of constituency attitudes. In the Labour Party, a candidate may bring herself to the attention of a local party in a number of ways, including an appearance on the central 'A' list of trade union-sponsored candidates, or on the 'B' list of other candidates approved by head office. At one time, the lists were more important than they are now. Candidates may nowadays be considered at preliminaries or at social occasions, but this tends to operate against women, who often lack the time and money to go along.

The trade union 'A' list also accounts for the dearth of women Labour candidates, since in 1979 women accounted for only 3 per cent of the names on it. One of the very few women M.P.s who came to Westminster via the trade union route, Joan Maynard, only became an M.P. after her union ambitions had been thwarted. Having constructed a local Labour Party branch in the Conservative area of Thirsk, North Yorkshire, and defeated such worthies as the chemist, the parson and the squire in local elections, she concentrated on working her way up the ranks of the Farmworkers' Union, her great love. She became its national vice-president in 1966, and it was only when she was stymied in her attempt to become president that she decided to pursue her commitment to the farmworkers by becoming an M.P. The tiny number of women who play an active part in trade unions, however, means that few women can follow Joan Maynard's example.

In the Conservative Party, a centralised selection procedure means that would-be candidates have to clear a number of central committee hurdles before constituencies see their details. Marcus Fox M.P., was the party's vice-chairman in charge of candidates for three years before the 1979 general election. During that time, he said, he let it be known that the party would be drawing its candidates from a wider base than hitherto, both in terms of sex and social class. It had worked, he said, because three years previously women had constituted rather less than 10 per cent of the total on the candidates' list, whereas at the 1979 election the proportion was approaching 15 per cent. 'A lot of the prejudice has been removed,' he said, 'but being an M.P. is a difficult job and only a limited number of women will be prepared to make the sacrifices necessary without the certainty of gaining selection or election.'

What did he look for in women who presented themselves for selection? 'They've got to have a certain toughness, be able to communicate, be able to convert people,' he said. 'They've got to have the charisma, the spark necessary in anybody who wants to succeed in politics, and if they can't convince me, they aren't going to convince the electorate. The interests of most of the ones I've seen are mainly domestic. If a woman had four kids under five and a husband on a very low income, we wouldn't suggest she should go in for it. If she had a young family, we would want to know what arrangements had been made for them. We can't lower our standards, or give the impression that any woman who applies will get on to the list.'

Both he and Angela Hooper, the Conservative Party's Chief Woman Executive, said that despite such efforts there was persistent hostility at constituency level towards women candidates. Miss Hooper, who used to be an area agent for the party, said that many constituencies preferred married male candidates because they reckoned that they then effectively secured two candidates for the price of one; they knew that the wives would do all the constituency work. Mr Fox thought that the biggest barrier to women candidates was put up by women party workers – a point of view shared by several women M.P.s. 'I'm surprised that as women have so much influence in the party, they don't influence the constituencies to select more women,' he said. On selection committees, after all, up to one third of the members could be women and this constituted a potentially powerful block vote.

Miss Hooper disagreed, however. 'When I see a selection committee predominantly composed of women I may accept that theory, but until then I'm not prepared to do so,' she said. 'Some committees start off with a list of prejudices. They'll say, we don't want a Catholic, we don't want a Jew, we don't want a bachelor and of course we don't want a woman.'

The figures speak for themselves. Less than 15 per cent of the people on the Conservatives' candidates' list in 1979 were women, and only 8.4 per cent of the Labour Party's 'B' list were women. And in the constituencies, although I found no one who was prepared to admit to prejudice, there was plenty of evidence of the obstacles that local parties put in the way of women. One Labour Party agent said that he had known constituencies where women simply didn't figure at all, except when it came to making the tea. A rather embittered Conservative woman, who had been short-listed for a candidacy but had failed to get it, said: 'There's still a very large number of people within the party who don't take women candidates seriously, even today. Men love a woman to be feminine; as soon as she appears to be on their intellectual level, she's no good. I have to be much better than a man, and this applies all the way through in politics. Making the tea and raising the funds are necessary, and there are women who are quite happy to do this. But it's also essential that women who now have two jobs and take a much keener interest in current affairs should have an outlet for expressing their views. Some constituencies say they will consider anything but a woman. Although women are the first to say we should have more women in Parliament, they will invariably vote for a dishy young man. I was once told to my face that a selection committee didn't want a woman candidate, and on another occasion I inferred it.'

But have attitudes changed at all over the years within the constituencies? The truth is more complicated than a simple diagnosis of continuing discrimination. Two recent phenomena make such a simple diagnosis difficult: the performance of women in the 1979 election to the European Parliament, and the relatively high proportion of women M.P.s sported in the past by the Scottish National Party. Particularly because it took place so soon after the abysmal performance of women in the British general election, the European election provided quite a shock. Women captured eleven out of eighty-one seats in the European election, a percentage of 13.5 – even though the percentage of women who stood was only 10.2. Yet in the general election, women candidates represented only about 8 per cent of the total, and the nineteen who were elected represented less than 3 per cent. One can only speculate about the reasons for this discrepancy, particularly as most of the women Euro-candidates had at some time nourished aspirations towards Westminster. Because the Euro-constituencies were so large, there was possibly less opportunity to measure the likely impact of a woman candidate on individual industrial or agricultural areas which might be thought to harbour prejudices against women. Or, more cynically, perhaps membership of the European Parliament was seen as less important than being a British M.P. There may also be less hostility towards women participating in something new and untried, whose benefits are not immediately apparent.

There is certainly less hostility towards women fighting hopeless Parliamentary seats, or representing parties that are either new or in the doldrums. The most dramatic example of this was provided by the Scottish National Party, which won twenty-two seats between 1945 and 1979, returning three women M.P.s among them – Margo MacDonald, Margaret Bain and Winifred Ewing (who won two separate seats). Apart from its women M.P.s, the S.N.P. also boasts a high proportion of women members and party activists. All this is even more remarkable given the old-fashioned attitudes towards women still prevailing in Scotland. But as the party became more successful, fewer women stood for Parliament. Conversely, since the Liberal Party has been in decline, it has selected a relatively high number of women to stand, though none has been elected since 1950.

For some women M.P.s, being a woman was a positive advantage because they attracted so much publicity in their first attempt to win a seat, far more than a young male hopeful would have enjoyed. The majority of women had to battle through a number of unsuccessful selection attempts, it is true, but a sizeable number appear to have experienced almost no difficulty in being selected. By and large, it was the Conservative women who felt that discrimination was only in the eyes of the women themselves, and that any good candidate worth her salt could get into Parliament if she tried hard enough. The one Labour exception who also subscribed to this doctrine of merit was Joan Lestor, who declared robustly that the notion that women with Parliamentary ambitions were disadvantaged was rubbish. Anyone could do it; she herself had been approached by people she had got to know in the Labour movement who asked her to stand; she'd won the selection at Eton and Slough, and there it was. 'A lot of rubbish is talked about women in Parliament,' she declared. 'Most women here have fallen into the place; either their families were involved in it, or else they knew people in the party. Any young woman in politics is at a distinct advantage; there are lots of young men around, but if you are a woman and are reasonably articulate and can state your case, you are noticed and remembered much longer. Women in the Commons are not that outstanding, because it's not that difficult to get in.'

Certainly, there are a number of examples to support Miss Lestor's point. Most women had made a name for themselves before they became M.P.s, either as party workers or, like Barbara Castle and Patricia Hornsby-Smith, by using the party conferences as a national platform to display their talents. Lady Bacon was known as a speaker at election meetings, and after only one unsuccessful selection conference was selected in 1938 for the Leeds North-east seat that she finally won in 1945. It had been a safe Conservative seat, with a majority of 12,000 in 1935, and her victory represented the biggest swing in the country. 'Sometimes it's an advantage to go to a selection conference as a woman, provided you don't stress the "woman" part; anyone who wants to be a "woman M.P." is doomed,' she said.

Baroness Emmet, a former Chairman of the influential Women's National Advisory Committee of the Conservative Party, had been the first woman and the first non-Parliamentarian to have been appointed a full member of the British delegation to the United Nations, complete with ministerial rank, in 1952. 'I could speak four languages and had experience and knew what I was doing,' she told me. 'A woman has to be better than the chaps, but you mustn't trade on it because if you do they won't like you. But once they've accepted you, they never want anyone else.' Born in 1899 and educated at Oxford, she became an M.P. in 1955 with apparent ease.

Neither Ann Taylor nor Oonagh McDonald, Labour M.P.s for Bolton West and Thurrock, had any difficulty in being selected. Ann Taylor first tried Bolton East, where she was well known as a local girl who helped out with her father at election times. But such familiarity, she felt, counted against her because it was difficult for people who had known her as a small child to take her seriously as a potential M.P. But three weeks after being turned down at Bolton East, she was selected for the sister constituency of Bolton West, where she was less well known. It was simply a case, she said, of being in the right place at the right time. Oonagh McDonald had even less difficulty at Thurrock, a safe Labour seat. 'I didn't know a soul in the area, but I just wrote in. I made a point of being straight about everything, and I think they just preferred my ideas.'

Helene Hayman benefited considerably from the publicity that invariably envelops a young, attractive, female candidate. Having been President of the Cambridge Union, she became known to the Labour Party in her home town of Wolverhampton through local newspaper coverage of the 'local girl makes good' variety. Backing a hunch, Wolverhampton South-west asked her to stand against the sitting Conservative member, Mr Enoch Powell. 'Violet Fletcher, the Mayor of Wolverhampton, said they wanted a gimmick to fight Powell,' Mrs Hayman told me. 'They wanted someone who would stand out and get some publicity, because it had always been such an uphill battle to fight against Powell.' The move turned out to be more successful than they could have anticipated, because at that February 1974 election, Enoch Powell declared he would be supporting the Labour Party and would be voting for Helene Middleweek, as she was then. 'I got a fantastic amount of publicity,' she recalled. 'It brought me the biggest swing in the country. It was an impossible election to fight because we had no organisation at all. It was the most ramshackle campaign, but we had every country's T.V. and radio and newspapers there. We couldn't have hoped for anything better.' Neither could she have hoped for a better boost to her political career, for after striking this publicity jackpot she was selected with ease for the Welwyn and Hatfield constituency later that year.

Yet Joan Lestor's analysis is not borne out by the experiences of many other women, who talk bitterly about the hopeless seats they were given to fight and who are in no doubt that at least part of their difficulty was the fact that they were women. Lady Vickers, for example, was the Conservative candidate for Poplar in London's East End in 1945, when she had the unenviable task of trying to persuade the local electorate to vote Conservative. She was given little help from the party to fight this hopeless seat; she conducted her campaign from an old sweetshop, which leaked, and when it rained she had to stick her umbrella up to protect her from the drips. And she was only selected at Plymouth, Devonport, she maintained, because it was seen as another hopeless seat – although she confounded everyone by winning it. 'It was obvious that there was prejudice,' she said. 'They wouldn't see me in constituency after constituency simply because I was a woman.'

Lady Pike, who won Melton Mowbray in 1956 for the Conservatives, came up against even more explicit prejudice. The party asked her to fight another woman, Harriet Slater, in Burslem, Staffordshire, but the selection committee there told her that the area was considered too rough for a woman candidate. There was, however, a marginal seat going at Leek, so perhaps she would care to try her luck there. At that point, someone interjected with the information that Leek had passed a resolution to say they would not select a woman. This strengthened Lady Pike's resolve, and as it happened Leek selected her.

She lost the election there, but when the Suez crisis of 1956 led to the resignation of Anthony Nutting from his Melton Mowbray seat the party asked Lady Pike to stand. She viewed the prospect with less than equanimity. 'I thought they wouldn't have a woman there of all places,' she said. 'It was a farming constituency, and it was far easier for a woman to get a city constituency. It was also a pretty tough fight over Suez, so I thought I didn't stand a chance. My mother had just died and it couldn't have been more inconvenient, but I was chosen and plunged straight into the by-election and won.' Not, though, before overcoming some vociferous opposition from people who protested that it was no use 'putting up a woman in these times to deal with Nasser, Dulles and those sort of people'. At her adoption meeting, she was reported to have told them that she did not pretend to be a farmer or a dairymaid, but she was a country woman who had worked hard to get the training and experience to become a candidate. This straightforward approach won the day.

Lady Hornsby-Smith, who won Chislehurst in 1950, had previously been turned down by Walthamstow on the grounds that a woman was not tough enough for the constituency. She encountered more subtle opposition at the Chislehurst selection conference. She was disconcerted to hear the chairman tell the candidates that they were not to assume that they were addressing an executive meeting, but to imagine it was a political meeting where 80 per cent of the audience were hostile. 'I was mad because I thought I wasn't going to get it,' Lady Hornsby-Smith told me. 'So I thought, right! If they are supposed to be opponents, opponents they will be. I referred to gentlemen with left-wing ideas, and I held forth as if I were speaking in the Gorbals. It went down very well.

'But when it came to the questions I had some really tough ones, far tougher, I later found out, than they asked the men candidates. For example, on the Education Bill, instead of asking for my view they asked for my opinion on a particular clause. It happened that I was the private secretary to Lord Selborne, who was piloting this Bill through the Lords, so I had had the Education Bill for breakfast, dinner and tea; so I was able to answer the question. They asked me directly whether I thought there was any disadvantage in being a woman, and I replied that I had managed to hold my own in areas like Ebbw Vale, Pontypool and Govan. At 1.15 that night the phone rang and a most miserable voice said, "Miss Hornsby-Smith, it's all right." I was so surprised, I said, "What the hell do you mean? You must be joking!" He said, "No, you've been selected" – and there was misery all through his voice!'

Margaret Jackson, who won Lincoln in 1974, was told to her face that under normal circumstances the Labour Party there would never have considered selecting a woman candidate; they had assumed it wasn't necessary, the situation had never arisen and they thought Lincoln didn't want a woman M.P. But in 1974 circumstances were far from normal. Dick Taverne, the former Labour member, had resigned the Labour whip and in a startling by-election in 1973 had been elected as the Independent Labour M.P. for Lincoln. 'Having lost the by-election, and with Taverne having a large majority, they decided they would have to have somebody distinctly different from Taverne, so they went for solid trade unionists or women,' Miss Jackson recounted wryly. The party asked Transport House to suggest women candidates and Margaret Jackson was recommended. When she arrived in the city, she realised that Lincoln lived by engineering, which made her, a trained metallurgist with factory floor experience, extremely suitable. The short list was whittled down to two women and two men trade unionists. 'The first question I was asked was whether I thought my sex would be a handicap to me in the factories. I relaxed at that point,' she said.

She was selected to fight the February 1974 election, which Dick Taverne won. She was aware that at that point the seat was quite hopeless, so she could hardly fail to do relatively well. 'I was conscious of the fact that Lincoln was a slightly old-fashioned city, that people wouldn't like a woman being bitchy, and I had to be careful about how I dressed and behaved. I was thirty-one, and conscious that I would be represented as a silly little girl who knew nothing. So I presented an image of gravity. Taverne's supporters said the Labour Party must be crazy, she's a kid, he'll wipe the floor with her. But I knew that, Lincoln being the sort of place it is and Taverne having been painted as Sir Galahad, the heroic figure and gentleman, he was in no position to attack me. He never worked out what to do about me without ruining his own image. In canvassing, I came to the conclusion that women do have a great advantage because once people decide to accept you, they almost adopt you.'

Some women ascribed their long struggles to get elected to the fact that they were women, but often it was clear that other issues had been involved. Jo Richardson, who fought four unsuccessful campaigns before becoming an M.P., has lost count of the total number of seats for which she applied. As a local councillor and secretary of the Tribune Group, she hardly lacked political contacts; but her frustrating experiences seem to have been caused by a combination of prejudice against women candidates and prejudice against her position on the left of the party. In Monmouth, after she had fought two elections there, the party told her they had come to the conclusion that a woman candidate didn't go down well in a rural seat. At both Hornchurch and Harrow East, which she fought in 1959 and 1964, the selection committees asked her if she saw any disadvantage in being a woman candidate – with the implication that the questioner thought there was.

But probably more important was the fact that she was not a supporter of the Labour leader, Hugh Gaitskell. In the early 1950s, she attacked Gaitskell in a speech to a meeting of Young Socialists at Hampstead. Candidates' nominations were at that time carefully in-spected by a party committee, and when her name came up for renewal on the list of candidates a few years later she was called for interview before a committee chaired by the M.P. Bessie Braddock. Seeing that she was about to be given the ideological third degree, Miss Richardson took out her notebook and pencil and prepared to take a note of what was said. 'But Bessie Braddock got aggressive and said no notes could be taken, and she closed the meeting there and then,' she recalled. 'So the issue went back to the organisation committee, with the information that the interview couldn't take place because I insisted on taking notes. A further interview was held, at which all that we discussed was the note-taking – nothing about me at all. After that, I was kept off the list until Gaitskell died.'

Making friends and influencing people clearly helps one get into Parliament, although most women M.P.s are coy about this side of their career, giving the impression that they were selected for their con-stituencies as complete unknowns. Lady White, however, was candid about her own selection for Flint. Having decided during the war that she wanted to become an M.P. and that she wanted to represent a Welsh constituency, she approached the women's organiser of the Labour Party to ask her how to start. She was told she wouldn't stand a chance in south Wales because the constituency parties there wouldn't look at a woman. There was only one Welsh constituency, Flintshire, which had not adopted a Labour candidate; it had a Conservative majority of 10,000 but one had to start somewhere. And she recommended, as a preliminary, a visit to Hugh T. Edwards, the Transport and General Workers Union regional organiser for north Wales, who was very active and influential in Labour Party circles. 'I went to see him, and we had a cup of tea together in a little cafe,' Lady White told me. 'I asked him whether he was looking for a candidate and he looked at me slightly quizzically, because I was an unknown young woman, although of course he knew my father and that was enough to place me as coming from a reputable background. I asked whether he really wanted the seat for himself. He burst out laughing, and said "My dear, if I really wanted to go to Westminster I wouldn't start in Flintshire." In due course, he invited me to meet some people and by the time they organised a proper selection conference in 1944 he had resuscitated some branches of the T.&G. and I got the nomination.' She reduced the Conservative majority to 1,000 and won East Flint in 1950.

Preparing the ground before a selection conference obviously pays dividends. Betty Boothroyd, who fought four unsuccessful campaigns before winning West Bromwich in 1973, recalled how she had felt it neccessary to woo the women of the area. One woman on the selection committee had told her that she couldn't ask the women of the town to vote for her since Miss Boothroyd was not married and so had never known what it was to have a hard life. She was advised to make her way into the Labour clubs in the area and see some of the wives of party workers. 'The implication was that they would influence their husbands. If the wives liked you, then you would be accepted and the husbands could like you. But if the husband was supporting a woman whom the wife had not seen or didn't like, the wife would become jealous.'

Only one woman has ever succeeded another woman as a constituency's M.P. Jill Knight followed Edith Pitt – although she was astonished at the reaction to her decision to apply for the selection. 'When Edith Pitt, whom I had known very well, died, I didn't immediately rush in because I think it's a terrible thing to do that as soon as someone dies,' she said. 'There were about 216 applications for that seat, so I knew I had heavy opposition. People knew me by then because, apart from coming from the area, I had done a lot of speaking at party conferences as I tried to learn all I could about my trade. But when I asked Geoffrey Johnson-Smith, who was then the deputy chairman in charge of candidates, about what I wanted to do, he said that I had no chance; having had one woman, they wouldn't want another to stand. I said to him, good grief, he wouldn't say they wouldn't consider another *man* because they already had one. I thought the whole thing was ridiculous – even though no woman had ever succeeded another woman before.'

If these women have anything in common, apart from their individuality, it is their stubborn determination and single-mindedness. Their careers are often testaments to strong wills that have overcome intimidating obstacles. Three women, two M.P.s and a former M.P. who is now a life peer, furnish striking examples of this. Elaine Burton, who became a Labour M.P. in 1950 and is now a peer, was born in 1904, the only child of an upper-class wastrel who had been a Olympic athlete and jockey. 'He was the waster of the family; he had no money, and was good at everything except work,' Lady Burton told me. 'None of my relatives worked; they all lived on their inherited wealth and my father wasted it all away.' She herself was a champion sprinter at sixteen years old and played cricket and hockey for Yorkshire. But she trained as an elementary schoolteacher and taught in Leeds for about eleven years, until the mid 1930s. Then she proceeded to uproot herself in a manner that could be described as either reckless or full of initiative.

'I realised that I wasn't going to get any further than a headmistress-

BARBARA CASTLE as Secretary of State for Employment and Productivity addressing the Labour Party Conference in Brighton, September 1969

BARONESS PHILLIPS, created a life Peer after the death in 1963 of her husband Morgan Phillips, General Secretary of the Labour Party. 'I put women first because I think they have no powerful voice, which puts them at the end of the queue. Who will speak for the deserted wives and widows?'

EIRENE WHITE, then a junior Minister at the Foreign Office, addressing the Labour Party Conference in Blackpool, October 1965. Her criticisms of Harold Wilson's policy on Rhodesia at the Party Conference the following year spoilt her chances of obtaining a Cabinet post

JUDITH HART
(above) and RENÉE
SHORT (below) at
the Labour Party
Conference in
Blackpool, September
1975

JO RICHARDSON
(right), Labour M.P.
for Barking. She
struggled for twenty
years to get into
Parliament

MAUREEN COLQUHOUN. After a
bitter fight against a move by her
constituency party to drop her, she was
defeated in the 1979 election. She claimed
that the adverse publicity about her
lesbianism had prejudiced her career

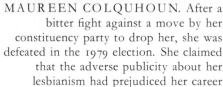

BARONESS ELLES, now a member of
the European Parliament. She is a qualified
barrister and has consistently worked for
women's rights, though she does not
consider herself a feminist. 'I took an
interest and did my best for my country,
but I couldn't have done what I do if I
hadn't been a kept woman. I live at my
home with my husband and don't
have to earn my way'

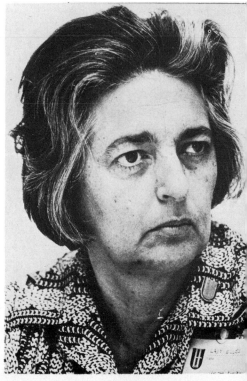

ship if I stayed in teaching, and I really am a political animal. I don't know necessarily that I'm a party person, but I'm rather drawn to causes. And without knowing why, in the early 1930s I became most anxious to know whether people who were unemployed didn't have jobs because there were no jobs or because they didn't want them. I decided to go to the Rhondda valley to investigate, but I had no means at all with which to do this.' So she enrolled as a welfare worker with the Council of Social Service and went to live with an unemployed miner and his family in the Rhondda. 'He hadn't worked for twelve years and their two sons, aged sixteen and seventeen, had never worked at all. I arrived at the very great conclusion that this was wrong! They had never had any holidays in their lives before. It seemed to me that the only way to do something about it was to get to London, although I never thought of getting into Parliament. It was very difficult at that time to come to London with no money and no influence; money mattered then, and you were too old to get a job at thirty.' But she came, and worked for a year raising money for a National Children's Home orphanage, a job that she hated. Hadn't she been worried about the risk she had taken in throwing up her teaching job in the middle of the Depression? 'It was a terrible risk that I took,' she admitted. 'And when I was working for the children's home, I used to think – my God, have I given up everything for this? But I was possessed by a burning desire to put the world to rights.'

The desire was to be put severely to the test. After leaving the children's home in relief, she found herself out of work for six months. 'I learned more about unemployment then than I had ever done during my whole time in the Rhondda valley,' she remembered ruefully. 'I didn't want to go back to teaching, so I went on the dole. Once you feel there isn't a place for you, you get almost desperate.' She eventually found work writing newspaper articles and working for a department store; meanwhile, her political interest had blossomed. She joined the Commonwealth Movement, whose main luminary was the writer J.B. Priestley, a leftish movement that thought it was a mistake for the Labour Party to refrain from fighting elections during the war. It introduced her to the excitement of fighting elections, since she fought West Hartlepool for it, and in 1944 she was selected to fight South Hendon for the Labour Party. 'I was bitterly disappointed, because we nearly won,' she said. 'In those days, I thought the best person always won and I thought that I was the best person!' She eventually won Coventry South, which she held for nine years. When she lost her seat the event desolated her. 'I lost everything, because I had lost my platform which was everything to me,' she said. In 1961 Hugh Gaitskell asked her to sit on a commission investigating the press. She took the opportunity of telling him that the thing she missed most in life was having a platform for her views, and at the end of that year he told her he was recommending her for a peerage. 'I really couldn't believe it,' she said. 'If I could have had the choice between thousands of pounds per year and a platform, I would have chosen the platform.'

Lady Burton showed considerable tenacity and independence in throwing up a safe, established career for a life of uncertainty and in embracing a political philosophy and way of life so unusual for an upper-class woman. Sheila Wright, who became a Labour M.P. in 1979, also rebelled violently against the political affiliations and way of life of her family. All her relatives were Conservatives and the family had a long history of serving in India, where Mrs Wright herself was brought up before the war. Her father was a policeman, and her mother did a lot of 'Lady Bountiful' social work, to use Mrs Wright's own words. India had a profound effect upon the young Sheila. 'I didn't like the extreme poverty, the results of the class and caste system that I saw,' she told me. 'I was there at the time of the Bengal famine, and that was the really traumatic influence. There were children dying all around you, but at the same time there were British and Indian society people going on with their entertainments. You could walk down the road to a ball and step over dying children. We were 2,000 miles away from Bengal, but we were still affected by the famine. Yet because only 20,000 people had died in our province, it was not considered a famine area because not enough had died. There was something wrong with that society.'

She joined the Indian army and ran a convalescent depot, and met a number of people who had come from England and whose politics were leftish. She returned to Britain immediately after the war and joined the Labour Party, because she felt she had to do something about the political situation. She went to live in Birmingham, where she was elected to the council and eventually became chairman of its education committee – which prompted the joke that she was the only education committee chairman who had never been to school. For as a child, she had received no formal education. Her mother had taught her to read and write when she was seven, but apart from less than eighteen months' tuition by unqualified governesses she simply taught herself by reading everything she could lay her hands on. When she arrived in Britain, however, she managed to get a place on a social science course at Southampton University as it was taking ex-service people on a generous basis. Later, she did an external degree in sociology at London University, and was proud of the fact that she gained an upper second.

She had been ambivalent about wanting to stand for Parliament, never viewing it as a serious possibility until 1964. Then, when she was six months pregnant, she was telephoned by the Labour Party in the Handsworth constituency of Birmingham who were desperate for a good candidate. They told her that everyone on their list was terrible, so they wanted to put her name forward. She fought the seat that year and in 1966, reducing the Conservative majority both times. She was selected again in 1970, but by then had experienced considerable personal difficulties. She had undergone three operations for cancer, and had been discharged from hospital shortly before the 1970 election after treatment for thrombosis which had left her blind in one eye. 'When it was a question of re-selecting for Handsworth, the doctor said I had to choose between council and work and Parliament because otherwise I would be dead,' she said. She chose the council, but in 1974, when the sitting M.P. retired, Mrs Wright was again re-selected and returned to the Parliamentary fray.

Mrs Wright rebelled against her upbringing and overcame the handicaps of a lack of formal education and, later, severe illness to become an M.P. But of all the women in Parliament, the story of Elaine Kellett-Bowman is perhaps the strangest. Until twenty years ago, her life was unremarkable. She read politics, philosophy and economics at Oxford, became a social worker, married Mr Charles Kellett, a farmer, and had four children. She nourished political ambitions which were encouraged by her husband. She recalled one political meeting in 1950 held in the local viallage hall near where they lived in Wales, where they went along to offer help during the general election. At the end of the meeting her husband, an exceedingly shy man, hurtled up to the front of the hall and urged the party workers to make use of his wife. So she spoke at public meetings and toyed with the idea that one day she might become an M.P.

In 1959 a personal tragedy interrupted her political ambitions, which by then had led her to fight one unsuccessful Parliamentary campaign. Mr Kellett was killed in a car crash, which almost killed her as well. She survived, but lost virtually her entire face and memory. Her face was restored; the plastic surgeon discovered a photograph of her on an election address in her handbag, she told me, and with the aid of that was able to build up her face again. But her memory was much more of a problem. She found herself trying to run her farm single-handed and bring up her four children – the eldest of whom was thirteen at the time – with no memory at all. 'If someone came to sell fertiliser, for example, I would order it again and again because I couldn't remember having done so already,' she recalled. She went to a specialist, who told her that a long holiday might possibly encourage her memory to return.

On the afternoon of her visit to the specialist, she went to a Women's Institute meeting, where she heard about a competition to find Britain's 'Number One Country Housewife'. The winner would tour the United States. Without further ado, Mrs Kellett-Bowman entered it – and won, despite her lack of memory. 'They asked me things like what I did in my spare time, and I couldn't remember,' she said, 'but if you're used to public speaking, that sees you through.' So she toured the U.S.A. as Britain's Number One Country Housewife, but she still returned without a memory. She was then advised that intense concentration might bring it back. So she enrolled on a correspondence course to read for the Bar, a course she studied at night after running the farm during the day. She got through both Roman and Constitutional Law in a month, and the concentration did the trick: her memory finally returned. 'It was a marvellous antidote to running a farm,' she remarked.

Not many women can emerge from widowhood, run a farm, raise four children, cope with illness, read for the Bar and become an M.P. Perhaps unsurprisingly, in view of her history and her political philosophy, Mrs Kellett-Bowman is scornful of those women M.P.s who emphasise the difficulties they have encountered in getting to Parliament. Anyone can do it if she is determined enough, she said. Sex discrimination, domestic commitments, all can be pushed aside by the right attitude of mind. But this stern doctrine of merit begs too many questions. There can be no doubt that there is still substantial prejudice towards women politicians. National party workers agree it is there; local constituency parties and associations admit it exists; many women M.P.s have either experienced it directly or feel sure that it has operated subtly against them. There is equally no doubt that certain combinations of personal circumstances and mental and physical qualities can overcome these prejudices; the experiences of all these women in Parliament, various as they are, testify to that. But these women are, in the main, people of exceptional toughness, strength of character, determination and – with one or two exceptions – intelligence. Most were elected to Parliament as a result of being in the right place at the right time, of knowing enough of the right people, of having used their time in local government or on party conference platforms to make their names. These factors are not, of course, peculiar to women politicians; but because of all the hoops through which they have to jump, and because of the many pressures upon them, women have to be one step ahead of men in everything. They have to be relatively more intelligent, more forceful, more conscientious; they have to make sure they are in the public eye and draw attention to themselves in a way that men do not. In the words of Barbara Castle, women in politics have to shake the men to the core.

4 *Three Outstanding Women*

AS Margaret Thatcher was being driven to Buckingham Palace to accept the task of forming a government, a twist of fate punched home with a vengeance the ironic nature of her victory. For the very seat that assured her of an absolute majority in Parliament fell to the Conservatives at that moment. The seat was Hertford and Stevenage, and the ousted M.P. was Shirley Williams, until then the Secretary of State for Education, and herself widely tipped as a potential Labour leader and Prime Minister.

When this news was conveyed to Mrs Thatcher, she must have felt that her triumph had been sealed with a symbolic flourish. For she regarded Mrs Williams with a mixture of admiration and irritation. She believed that Mrs Williams was the only woman in the 1974-79 Parliament worthy and capable of Cabinet rank apart from herself. She respected her intellect and her integrity, but in the comparisons she obviously drew between herself and her Labour rival she seemed to conclude that she had more justification for pride. Shirley, she seemed to be saying, had always had it made and had never had to struggle. She, Margaret, on the other hand, had had to fight her way up the meritocrat's ladder from humble beginnings to a place in the middle-class political élite. It was almost like a schoolgirl's pettishness, saying that the brightest girl in the class had only got top marks because she had had help at home from her parents. And to add insult to injury, Shirley, who had never had to dirty her hands, was apparently revered and loved by almost everyone; even her political opponents found it hard to speak ill of her. But she, Margaret, was regarded with something less than affection and was even mocked and reviled for embracing the middle-class way of life that Shirley had taken for granted.

Margaret Thatcher's triumph and Shirley Williams's defeat were the two ends of a seesaw, whose previous equilibrium had now given way to a violent movement for change which had cast one of the players out of the Parliamentary game. But a third figure, who must be considered alongside these two women, had already chosen to slip into the shadows before the upsets of 4 May. Barbara Castle, considered by many to have been the most outstanding woman in Parliament since the Second World War, had announced that she was retiring from British politics – although with characteristic brio, she had also determined to stand for the European Parliament, where she is now the leader of the British Labour members. So by the end of 4 May Britain had gained its first woman Prime Minister but had lost from the Parliamentary scene its only other female contender for the post and its most distinguished postwar woman parliamentarian.

All three women had been plagued constantly by speculation about their chances of holding the top government post. All three had said that the chances of a woman becoming Prime Minister in their lifetime were remote – and they wouldn't particularly want the job anyway. As a corollary to such speculation – which came about because they were seen as the three most outstanding women in British politics – all of them developed public images which made them appear larger than life. These images developed an almost mythological quality, and anecdotes abounded – and still do – to reinforce the particular characteristics which are seen to remove them from the sphere of the ordinary and commonplace.

Shirley Williams' 'niceness' has been so magnified that one is constantly amazed that such a paragon of virtue ever became part of the shabby business of politics at all, let alone an achiever of high office. Barbara Castle's emotion and temper are legendary, as are Margaret Thatcher's opposite qualities of ice and steel. How far these characteristics are true reflections of the personalities of these women, and how far they have been exaggerated to maintain images eagerly accepted by a public that requires an element of theatre from its politicians, is difficult to disentangle.

Personalities are obviously decisively influenced by background and upbringing, but how far did the backgrounds of these three women determine the pattern of their successful political lives? Was it inevitable, given their family circumstances, that they should have gone into politics, and chosen the political parties that they did? Margaret Thatcher would not grant me an interview, and so I was unable to ask her the question directly. Nevertheless, from interviews she has given in the past and from a number of other published sources, it is possible to construct some fascinating comparisons between herself, Mrs Williams and Mrs Castle. If there are some striking differences between their family environments, there are some even more startling similarities.

All three were daughters of parents who were, in their different ways, formidable and exceptionally powerful characters. All three had fathers who were passionately interested in politics, and in the case of Mrs Williams her mother was involved as well. Barbara Castle's father, Frank Betts, was a socialist pioneer in Bradford who had to conceal the fact that he edited the local socialist newspaper because of his position as an income tax inspector. Her great-grandfather on her mother's side, Banks Ferrand, ran, albeit unsuccessfully, as a parliamentary candidate for Stafford in 1886. 'His election manifesto on the need to reform all proved abuses (which I've still got) would do credit to Michael Foot,' his great-granddaughter commented admiringly more than 100 years later.

Shirley Williams's father, Professor George Catlin, stood for Parliament as a Labour candidate in 1931 and 1935; both were bad years for Labour candidates, and he was unsuccessful. He was asked to stand again in 1945, but he was also offered the chance of a position abroad and, as he was certain that Churchill and the Conservatives would be returned, he did not take up the offer. Had he done so, he would probably have been elected in the Labour landslide of that year and Shirley Williams's career might have taken a quite different path.

Margaret Thatcher's father, Alfred Roberts, who ran two grocery shops in Grantham, Lincolnshire, stood as an independent on the local council and rose to become an Alderman and then Mayor. Party politics at that time were more remote from local government than they are today, but he was a Conservative, although he had been brought up in a Liberal family. The Conservatives, he felt, stood for what the Liberals had represented in his own father's time.

Mrs Williams feels certain that the political interests of their parents constituted a decisive factor linking her own career with those of Mrs Castle and Mrs Thatcher. 'All of us had this same characteristic – parents who were frustrated M.P.s,' she told me. 'All these parents saw their daughters as carrying out their ambitions because they had no alternative – either they had no sons, or else their sons were not interested in politics. I have a brother, for example, but he is not interested.'

Yet although all three came from political families, the nature of their political involvement was not the same at all. Mrs Williams came from a highly cosmopolitan and intellectual background where political interest embraced the whole world and not just the issues of the day in Britain. Her father, a political scientist, was publicly somewhat overshadowed by her mother, Vera Brittain, a renowned feminist author and passionate pacifist. She was a prolific writer and lecturer and was heavily involved in the Peace Pledge Union and Save Britain Now. Her books earned the distinction of being burned by the Nazis at Nuremberg, and both she and George Catlin were on the Gestapo's black list of people who would need to be eliminated if the Nazis invaded Britain – a fact which saved her reputation, since as a pacifist Vera Brittain was viewed by the Home Office as a potential quisling.

As if all this political activity were not enough, the family also had living with them Winifred Holtby, the feminist writer and great friend of Vera Brittain. Shirley Williams recalls that she was very wrapped up in the early movements of the African National Congress; the family house in Chelsea saw a procession of African guests, as well as others concerned with the movement for black independence. They also took in a number of Jewish refugees, mainly writers, from Hitler's Germany. Bits of the world, indeed, moved through that Chelsea drawing room, just as Lady Eden was later to complain that Suez flowed through hers. So Shirley grew up in a family that took political activity for granted and accepted politicians as a regular part of the furniture. At five years old, she was dandled on Pandit Nehru's knee; at fifteen she was taken to Transport House to join in the victory celebrations after the 1945 general election. She herself comments: 'Although I had a very broken up childhood geographically, all through there was this very strong thread of involvement in politics at the grass roots level. I was brought up in an atmosphere of intensive combativeness directed against Nazism and to a certain extent imperialism and so I was suffused in politics from the word go.' All this led to a certain precocity in her political development: 'When I was four I was pushed in a push chair around the streets of Sunderland where my father was standing as the Labour

candidate in the admittedly hopeless election of 1935, and occasionally I
was pinched in order to say loudly, "Vote for Daddy!" '

Barbara Castle was also brought up in a family atmosphere of intense
political activity – her family being centred around the overwhelming
personality of her father, who was both adored and feared. Like Shirley
Williams, her earliest memories are of a house full of political visitors.
'One of my earliest memories, in fact, is of other people's children eating
and sleeping in the house: in the 1920s the children of miners on strike;
in the 1930s Spanish refugees. There always seemed to be someone
sleeping on the sofa,' she told Kenneth Harris of the *Observer* on 28
August 1969. Her father ran a kind of intellectual salon to which people
would come for conversation about politics, literature or art. One of his
protégés was Vic Feather, then a van boy but later to become General
Secretary of the T.U.C. and a life peer. 'There would be a sort of
continual open forum and Vic would come round to discuss art and get
his reading lists,' Mrs Castle recalled. 'Bradford in the 1920s was such a
live place, a place of ideas, of tough, real political argument: a very good
training ground.'

Unlike Vera Brittain, Mrs Betts, Barbara's mother, was not an
intellectual woman or renowned in her own right. Mrs Castle remembered affectionately: 'But underneath the daintiness she had
tremendous stamina, which she got from her mother – an indomitable
little woman of really tough working-class stock. And she had an
instinctive emotional response to new and challenging ideas.' She
followed adoringly where her charismatic husband led, since he was the
unquestioned star of the family. 'He was the most bookish man I've ever
met,' Mrs Castle said. 'Books, ideas, literature, painting, discussion were
his life.' She described him as richly Rabelaisian, yet with an intensely
puritanical streak; an iconoclast who broke completely with his own
home background but was scathing about anything his family did that
he thought was wrong. 'He didn't give a damn for his appearance or
what anyone thought of him; he took a puckish delight in shocking
people with his ribaldries. Yet if we did anything he thought cheap he
was down on us like a ton of bricks. When I was at Oxford I started
having ambitions like everyone else about going out into the world and
making money and I rashly mentioned it to him. "Oh, money," he said in
a tone of contempt I shall never forget, "if it's money you're interested in
..." I felt like a pygmy. He had a foul temper and a streak of cruelty that
we used to rage against yet the impression he has left on me is of total

generosity and tenderness for the world, a religious impression even though he became a rationalist. I learned to believe in the power, especially the therapeutic power, of the truth. Dad hated hypocrisy. He wanted us to use knowledge to get things changed, to revolutionise social values. For him, to be good was to do good.'

The family atmosphere was one of intense political debate. Socialism was seen to stand for alleviating not just financial poverty but spiritual poverty and cultural starvation as well. Barbara Castle's political precocity took a rather more active and direct form than that of Shirley Williams. At six years old, she wrote her first political address: 'Vote for me and I will build you houses.' At eight, she acted in a production of Galsworthy's *Strife*, one of the first plays about class warfare, before an audience of unemployed miners. She told Paul Johnson in the *Daily Mirror* on 26 July 1968: 'They sat on hard wooden benches priced tuppence a seat. They were undernourished and defeated men. I can't forget their white faces staring at me over the footlights.' She herself says that her father was one of the biggest influences on her life. 'At first I was overawed by him but gradually I steeled myself to disagree. And I held my own. He had a hot temper and he was a great egoist. But he had an absolutely unqualified integrity and a high standard of personal conduct. That background, I think, is one reason for the impression I give of being belligerent and intransigent and all that.'

Margaret Thatcher's family, although also politically involved, was very different from that of Mrs Williams or Mrs Castle. Her background was very much narrower; the Roberts family enjoyed a social position, but only in Grantham. Margaret's father was a pillar of the local community, but his house was not full of political refugees and visiting statesmen. Nor, apparently, was it full of ordinary people. 'There was a road near our home where people like that lived and I used to walk along it. So I know what they're like,' she once remarked. Dole queues were something she observed only at a distance, although she remembers the father of one friend of hers who was unable to find work for a long time. How different her world was from that in which Shirley Williams was brought up was vividly illustrated by a B.B.C. radio interview, when she reminisced about the thirties and forties. 'I remember my sister had a German correspondent and suddenly we got a letter. The girl was a Jew and could we help her out! And there was a political problem right in our home! Right in our home!' But this was an isolated, remote experience. Mrs Williams, who was also on the programme, pointed out that this was the sort of life in the middle of which she lived all the time.

Like Mrs Castle, Mrs Thatcher feels she owes much to her father. But she is less warm towards her mother. She told the *Daily Telegraph* in 1975: 'My father was a wonderful man. He made me read widely and for that I owe him everything. I loved my mother dearly but after I was fifteen we had nothing more to say to each other. It wasn't her fault. She was weighed down by the home, always being in the home.' Her father was a stern man who left school when he was thirteen; he was determined that his children should have the advantages that he himself had never enjoyed. He was described by the town librarian as 'the most skilled debater the council ever had'. His grocery shop became a centre of conversation about current affairs, since councillors and others used to drop in all the time; Mr Roberts frequently sought Margaret's opinion and used to take her around with him. He was a religious man, a teetotal Methodist lay preacher who combined compassion towards people's personal problems with a belief that people should be encouraged to stand on their own feet. Mrs Thatcher recalled: 'He had done that himself. He had worked in somebody else's shop and had saved enough to buy a shop of his own. My mother, too, was much the same. She was a dressmaker. She had stood on her own feet, too. Their parents before them. This has had its effect on me.'

The Roberts family, being prosperous small shopkeepers, seems to have fallen into that curious no man's land in the class system which defies an easy stereotype. Some have concluded that Margaret was brought up in conditions approaching social deprivation because they lived above the shop, and that the family was working class; others have sourly observed that as her father owned not one but two grocery shops he was well on the way to being considered a small-time property magnate and the family was therefore middle class. Neither conclusion takes into account the subtle nuances of the English class system, under which a man's ostensibly humble occupation as a grocer can exist side by side with his standing as his town's first citizen. Margaret seems to have embodied the paradox. A woman who was her contemporary at school remarked: 'She was very aware of the position her family held in the town's society and was condescending to many girls.' Yet at the same time she aspired to join the middle class, and once remarked that the charm of Britain lay in the ease with which one can move into this prized circle.

Mrs Thatcher herself recalled to Kenneth Harris on 5 October 1975 that her childhood was comfortable. 'Thousands of children were having a very hard time of it in the late 1920s and early 1930s, but I was not. We did not live extravagantly, indeed we couldn't, but I was never short of necessities at a time when some children were.' The privations she suffered, perhaps, were mental rather than physical ones. Her father's strict insistence on effort, and disapproval of pleasure, may have spurred her on to a first-rate academic education but seemed to take little account of the fact that education is a far broader process of assimilation. 'Pleasure' – going to dances and meeting people, for example – can be extremely educative. Yet she was discouraged from this until she freed herself by going to university, when she went to a dance for the first time. Social life in Grantham was confined to church functions.

She commented to Kenneth Harris on her home life: 'There was a great sense of effort, of always doing something. Not necessarily work – talk, discussion, playing the piano – but always something. You worked hard, not because work was everything but because work was necessary to give you what you wanted. There was also the feeling that idleness was a waste. You worked hard at school, not only to improve your mind but to enable you to get a job that was interesting and demanding. It was very important to use your life to some purpose. The more you put into your life the more you would get out. To pursue pleasure for its own sake was wrong.' Her father believed firmly in right and wrong and in the importance of character, formed by hard work. But his daughter's character must have been limited by such a restricted environment. 'I had never gone abroad and considered a day trip to Nottingham a great treat,' she once said of her teenage years. 'I preferred the company of adults and talked politics with my father's friends when they came to the house. That is how my interest in a political career really began.'

Yet when it came to the kind of education that can be gathered from books, Margaret's father was passionately keen that his children should make full use of this in order to give themselves the opportunities he had never had. In this, he was at one with Barbara Castle's father, who was also a fervent believer in the merits of self-education. Mrs Thatcher recalled in a radio interview: 'One of my Saturday morning jobs was to go to the local library and get two of the latest books, one on political affairs and the other a biography. We all read them. They were very interesting times; the thirties and forties were more packed with interest than any period since.' Mr Roberts' educational zeal didn't stop at books but took in music and lectures as well; anything that had an educational content was desirable. At five years old, Margaret was accordingly sent to take piano lessons; later she was taken along to current affairs talks by visiting lecturers.

Barbara Castle's father made every book in his sizeable collection available to his children as soon as they could read, so that it became a point of principle for them to read everything they could lay their hands on. She commented: 'The whole of family life was dominated by the fact that he had to have his study and his books. He always read at meals – right through them. We were not allowed to speak. Then in our teens we graduated into saying, "I don't agree with you, Dad." '

One gets the impression, however, that reading and associated cultural pursuits were so much taken for granted by Shirley Williams' parents that they were more concerned with giving their children an education that accorded with their socialist – and feminist – ideals. Her mother, after all, was in the business of writing books, not merely reading them. So although they were a well-off professional couple, they deliberately chose to send Shirley to the local elementary school. 'Because they thought it was at a very early age, seven or eight, that you would absorb some understanding of the world you lived in, the society you lived in,' remarked Mrs Williams in a radio interview in 1973. 'Of course, the children were very badly off: I remember the L.C.C. used to give everybody paper dolls at Christmas and for quite a lot of the children that was all the Christmas presents they ever had. And I had to pretend that I lived downstairs in the cellar of our house because I didn't dare in that atmosphere admit I lived on the first floor. And that bit very deep, I think, into my consciousness. I think it had a lot to do with my remaining in the party my parents belonged to.'

This school was one of a total of eight she attended in her progressive, eccentric and peripatetic education in Britain and the United States. In an interview in the *Guardian* in 1971, she confessed: 'I didn't like school. I didn't go for the discipline. I also needed to get away from home, to go somewhere where no one knew my parents.' Barbara Castle, who had a far more conventional education, was also made to feel that she was different from her schoolmates; but whereas Shirley felt that she was too grand, Barbara was ostracised at her good girls' school for her Labour allegiance – a rather daring allegiance in the 1920s. She remembered: 'In 1929 I stood in a mock election. The daughters of the rich Bradford wool merchants voted me down. I only got seventeen votes out of 600. But in the real election we won all four Bradford seats. I went to school the next morning in triumph.'

It obviously required an unusually staunch character to espouse the unfashionable and derided Labour cause at a school where the very subject of politics was thought not quite genteel. Mrs Castle recalled: 'Those who were Labour were just a handful at school so we were having to stand out against the crowd and be jeered at because we were interested in politics, which wasn't considered quite ladylike by some of my friends.' Yet she can't have been so very ostracized, because she ended up becoming head girl – an achievement she later made light of by saying that she thought they were trying to make the poacher into the gamekeeper.

Like Shirley and Barbara, Margaret Thatcher was obviously a clever girl whose parents wanted to give her. the best education they could provide; the fact that the three were daughters rather than sons seems to have made no difference to any of the parents' ambitions for their girls. Indeed, Mrs Thatcher has agreed that her father saw in her a way of realising his own ambitions. But whereas Shirley Williams felt marked out by her social class and the renown of her parents, and Barbara Castle felt isolated through her political views, Margaret Thatcher seems to have been notable at school by virtue of her own personality. She was undoubtedly clever at school, a fact which she has never attempted to conceal. When asked a few years ago in what subjects she had been top of the form at school, she replied without a smile, 'Pretty well everything'.

But it was by no means an effortless cleverness, a quest for knowledge for its own sake; it was a relentless, even ruthless, driving forward to meet the standards set by her father. She once told a friend that her father would not tolerate excuses such as 'I can't' or 'I don't think I can manage it' or 'It's too difficult'. Everything was seen as a challenge, and she just had to cope with everything; if it was difficult, there was all the more reason for doing it. Fortunately, she had a good enough brain to enable her to meet her father's standards, but the extraordinary motivation behind her efforts produced a single-mindedness and belief in her own merit which now appear unattractive and unusual in a schoolgirl. There was, for example, her celebrated remark at the age of nine when she was congratulated on winning a poetry reading prize. 'I wasn't lucky, I deserved it,' the young meritocrat is reported to have said. She later remarked that at sixteen years old she came to the conclusion that she could get out of life absolutely anything that she wanted; the only trouble was deciding what she wanted. She was determined to get to university, and was furious with the teacher who wanted her to stay on at school for an extra year to prepare for the Oxford scholarship. In the teeth of all such advice, she crammed a five-year Latin course into a year to reach the required standard for the entrance exam – and typically got top marks in it.

Accounts of her childhood present her as a girl of rigid self-control who channelled all her talent and formidable energy into a carefully designed master plan in which whatever she did was worked out in advance as offering the best opportunities. She decided to study chemistry at Oxford because she realised that there was a great future in plastics, and was determined to get into that field before it became overcrowded. At seventeen she was advised by Norman Winning, the Recorder of Grantham and a friend of her father's, that her planned course of chemistry at Oxford would fit her for a career at the patent Bar – a career she accordingly decided to take up.

In sharp contrast, the young Barbara Castle was possessed by a sense of her own inadequacies and frequently dissolved into tears because she considered that she wasn't a 'raving beauty'. 'My problem was a very common one: a sense of inferiority,' she told Kenneth Harris. 'When I was a girl I had a tremendous feeling of inadequacy. I thought I was unattractive and thought no man would ever look at me. And later I thought I would never be any good at a job. I was full of anxieties. The only thing that gave me release was a challenge. I had courage, the kind of courage that goes with desperation and needs hostility to bring it out. When people said, "Of course you can do it, Barbara", I wilted, I got worse. But if they said, "You can't do it, you're hopeless," I saw red and damn well did it.'

All three women were involved in political life as children, and all three played prominent parts in university politics, but only Barbara Castle says that she always knew, from her earliest days, that what she really wanted to be was an M.P. Shirley Williams joined the Labour Party when she was fifteen, at about the time of her first serious involvement with politics, in the 1945 general election. But by then she had already been befriended by Herbert Morrison, then Home Secretary, who was, in Mrs Williams' opinion, the only man in the party who ever made a point of acting as a political patron to young women and taking them under his wing. She told me: 'I met him in an air raid shelter when I was thirteen. I got to know him quite well and he half adopted me. He used to invite me to have dinner with him at the Home

Office. He said to me, it takes a lot of courage for a man to encourage a young woman to go into politics because it could be misunderstood. Most men would not want the publicity. Even more than they are now, men were reluctant to put themselves into that position.'

She ran errands for the local party in the 1945 election, just as Mrs Thatcher had helped out in Grantham ten years previously, when she was ten years old. 'I do remember the 1935 election because we happened to know our local M.P.,' Mrs Thatcher recalled on radio. 'I was a runner between the election rooms and the polling booths to get the lists of the people who had voted. It was very exciting.'

All three were active in politics at Oxford, Shirley Williams and Margaret Thatcher becoming chairman of the Labour club and president of the Conservative Association respectively. Barbara Castle flung herself into Labour club politics at least partly as an escape from the university environment, in which she felt ill at ease. She found the other girls immature; the milieu didn't seem real to the girl who had been exposed to so many adult influences in Bradford. 'I felt I'd come from a very adult society to a superior girls' boarding school,' she later remarked. Her fellow students seemed to her to represent an unattractive mixture of adolescent personalities and over-developed academic knowledge.

Barbara was certain that she wanted to be an M.P. and everything she did after leaving university played second fiddle to her political ambitions. Shirley was far more ambivalent. She seemed to be drawn into politics more and more deeply, and not unwillingly, yet at the same time constantly debating in her own mind whether this was really what she wanted to do. At Oxford, she led quite a dizzy life, apart from her Labour club activities. She became features editor of the university magazine, *Isis,* which also proclaimed her an Isis Idol, and she acted prolifically. She fell in love, reputedly, as often as possible, and almost had her scholarship taken away. After she came down, she did some postgraduate work in the United States, worked as a journalist on the *Daily Mirror* and *Financial Times,* and taught at the University of Ghana. Meanwhile, she had been on the executive of the Labour youth section, had worked as an agent in the 1950 election 'because I was too young to stand as a candidate', and was a speaker in the election campaign of 1951. At the tender age of twenty-three she was adopted for Harwich. But she was racked by indecision.

'All this time I wasn't clear that I wanted to be in politics,' she told me.

'I was torn between politics and journalism. The first seat was hopeless. The people in the party knew me; I wasn't just appearing out of the blue. They knew it was hopeless and they were probably very glad to find a candidate at all. I wanted to fight it and discover what it was like to fight an election.' She has also said that the reason she stood for Harwich was that the chairman of the local party was a friend and asked her to. 'It was more that politics found me than me them,' she said. She fought Harwich twice before fighting Southampton Test in 1959. 'That was a very marginal seat, and there were some objections to me. Some people said it was a dockers' seat, and so would a woman be appropriate. Two or three members thought it wouldn't be a good idea, but they didn't prevail.'

After failing to win this seat, she took over as general secretary of the Fabian Society from William Rodgers, an old university friend. She widened the membership, which mainly consisted of young Gaitskellites, to include scientists and trade unionists, and eventually founded the Young Fabians, attracting considerable publicity all the while. The *Guardian* commented on 8 March 1960 that she was one of Hugh Gaitskell's brightest hopes. 'She made a stir at Blackpool in December when, after other delegates had made slashing attacks on the leadership she reminded the Labour Party Conference that domestic strife of this kind could only let in the Conservatives every time. Besides being learned about the Common Market and industrial efficiency she looks attractively unlike the idea of a woman Fabian propagated by, say, Mr Osbert Lancaster.'

She was then successful at Hitchin, which she won in 1964 and held until she moved over to Hertford and Stevenage in 1974. 'By the time I got to Hitchin I was already quite an experienced fighter. The by-elections had gone quite well, so they couldn't really say that there was evidence against me as a woman. Hitchin was a seat with a big new town in it, a lot of the old attitudes were going, so in a way the attitudes there were somewhat different to the rest of the country.'

Twenty years before Shirley Williams started on her path to Westminster, Barbara Castle had launched herself on the same route, but with single-minded determination. When she came down from Oxford, in the dog days of the 1930s, she was not lucky in finding employment. She got a job on a newspaper which folded within the week. She was unemployed for a while, then became a sales demonstrator for a firm of wholesale grocers in Manchester – an experience she later described as 'the most miserable year of my life'. She moved to London, where she worked as both a civil servant and a journalist. But all the time she was pegging away at developing a political career, reading Blue Books and White Papers and joining her local Labour party at St Pancras. For her the importance of academic knowledge lay in its potential usefulness in day-to-day life. 'I'm interested in all knowledge that can be used,' she told me. 'My Oxford special subject was monetary theory. I read it because I knew it was difficult and a challenge but also because I knew it was important and could be used.'

'I always wanted to be an M.P.,' she went on. 'Some people are political animals and I responded to the environment of a political family and it was my one ambition. When I came down to London and got active in the party in St Pancras, I was active and vocal at general management committee meetings and so I got selected as a council candidate and got on to the local authority. It was a step towards Parliament; any training was useful. It was political activity and it was all experience, although I enjoyed it for itself. Yet it wasn't enough in itself, but there wasn't much hope at the time of getting a parliamentary seat. This was the 1930s, after all, when the formation of a national government had clamped down and the Labour movement was laid flat on its back.' Even on the local council, however, she made sure that she was not shunted off into the placid areas considered suitable for a woman – health, welfare and education. 'I was always interested in economic and industrial matters. They wanted to put me on to the maternity committee, but I said I hadn't got any children! Anyway, I wanted to go on to Highways and Public Works. I've always been tremendously interested in what makes society tick. Sewage, for instance, is the most important element of urban life. I was put on to the Metropolitan Water Board and that fascinated me – how you kept a vast metropolis supplied with water.'

Her lucky breaks were provided by the Labour Party Conferences, which gave her a platform and from which she could make her name. She was sent as a delegate in 1933 and again in 1943, when she made a striking speech that hit the headlines and caught the popular imagination. 'Young people are tired of being told about jam tomorrow. They want jam today!' proclaimed the young Barbara Betts. It was the turning point in her life in more ways than one; it effectively provided her with a parliamentary seat, a political mentor and a husband.

She met the latter two almost in the same moment. Ted Castle, a journalist on the *Daily Mirror*, went to that 1943 conference and the first people he met there said to him, 'Did you hear Barbara Betts?' He asked who she was and was told she was 'a girl from St Pancras'. She met him, and almost at the same moment she met Nye Bevan, who had come up to congratulate her on her speech. She married Ted Castle the following year, a marriage which she always regarded as a crucial and stabilising element in her life. He died in 1979. 'Politics and marriage have achieved my ambitions and solved my problems inseparably; politics alone couldn't have, marriage alone couldn't have,' she once said. As for Aneurin Bevan, he was a huge influence on her political life. 'It wasn't that we were pals, it was that Nye was an enthuser, an inspirer of ideals, philosophies, standards and values. When I first came into politics I adored him from afar and Nye\was an enormous influence on me.'

Her success at the 1943 conference undoubtedly helped her secure the nomination for the seat at Blackburn, which she won two years later. When the 1945 election was called, she told me, she went straight into the business of trying to get a seat. 'It wasn't a very typical period, so many of the lads were away at the front and there had been such disruption of political activity. I remember some local parties were filling seats at the last minute.' She was nominated by the women's section of the Blackburn party, who wanted a woman on the short list. Characteristically, she injects a note of drama into her account of her selection. 'When I went to the selection conference I was in a wonky state from appendicitis; the doctor had said I wasn't to go, but I said I was. I was very shaky and when I got to my feet I said there were two things I wanted them to forget about me: one, that I was a woman, and two, that I was just out of hospital, and they should judge me as a socialist. The thing to do with patronising questions is to forestall them. You must never be on the defensive; never aggressive, always positive. I was lucky because I got a seat which was never safe but it always had a broad industrial base and a local bias towards the Labour Party, so I could build on it.'

Margaret Thatcher's progress to Parliament was rather more enigmatic. In the main, she has declared that in spite of her interest in politics as a teenager she never entertained any thoughts of becoming an M.P. until she went to university. The Oxford University Conservative Association, she told Ian McIntyre in a radio interview in 1973, gave a tremendous stimulus to her interest in politics, because of the contact it provided with all the active politicians of the day. 'And I saw the fascination of the life – and politics is a fascination, it's one of the most compelling things.' She spent most of her days working in laboratories, with lectures in the early evenings, and most of her spare time discussing politics – a far cry from the dizzy social life enjoyed at Oxford by Shirley Williams.

But Mrs Thatcher maintained in that interview that she always saw politics as a part-time activity, to be indulged in only at local level. 'I didn't think I'd have any chance to come in and be an M.P. in those days; I had to earn my own living because I had no money and M.P.s were only paid £400 a year and I couldn't see any prospect either of getting a seat or of living on what M.P.s were then paid. So I knew I'd have to work for quite a long time.' But then, it seems, she experienced a positively Pauline revelation. 'After a local dance one evening, we were having a discussion in the kitchen – I was about nineteen or twenty – when all of a sudden someone said, well, I suppose what you're really saying is that you'd like to go into Parliament. It was the first time the ambition had occurred to me.'

At least one rather sour acquaintance has scoffed at this account, on the grounds that Margaret always planned every stage in her develop-ment with great care and never decided anything on the spur of the moment. Certainly, this possibly apocryphal account does not square with a remark she herself made to the *Daily Telegraph* on 17 July 1970: 'I knew that I could not afford to go in for politics without some profession to back me up. That is why I went to university.' She is said to have told a friend at Oxford that she had two ambitions: to marry a rich man, and then to have a successful career in politics. (If she did say this, she would have been contradicting one of her father's guiding principles; as she recalled: 'Money was not as important as character. There are many things which ought never to be done for money – marriage, for instance. Money was only a means to an end. Ends never justified means.') Whether or not she said it, this is exactly what she did. In 1946 she represented OUCA at the Conservative Party Conference, as she did again in 1948, where she met a friend, one John Grant, who happened to be talking to the chairman of the Dartford Conservative Association, John Miller. Miller mentioned that they were looking for a candidate, prompting Grant to inquire whether they would consider a woman.

Miller was not enthusiastic about the idea, since Dartford was an industrial seat, but Grant pushed and Margaret got the nomination. Mrs

Thatcher recalled to Ian McIntyre: 'At the beginning I was extremely lucky. I had a very difficult seat to fight, Dartford and Erith, with a 20,000 Socialist majority. There were twenty-nine others against me, but one was different, and it was quite a good idea to have someone different in those circumstances. When I came to go in for one of the better seats, I well remember one of the women who had been on the selection committee saying to me "Mrs Thatcher, we thought you were extremely good but a large number of women in the audience felt that as you had young children you really ought not to be thinking of going into politics at all at the moment." '

For by the time Mrs Thatcher was selected for the Conservative plum of Finchley, she had married Denis Thatcher, the director of a paint company, whom she had met at Dartford, and had given birth to twins. Mr Thatcher subsequently sold his firm to an oil company and later became a director of Burmah Oil. There is no doubt that having such substantial financial backing made a considerable difference to Mrs Thatcher's career prospects. It enabled her to read for the Bar; it allowed her to employ a nanny to look after the twins and so freed her from domestic ties; it enabled her to meet all the expenses of getting into Parliament. She herself recognised all these things – although she could not understand why this aspect of her life did not go down well with the public and the press.

She told Taya Zinkin of the *Guardian* on 23 February 1962: 'I do not have to worry about money. As you know, we get no pension as of right. This can matter to those who have to support themselves. It's expensive to be in politics; one has to be mobile, one has to be well-groomed and one has to entertain.' But she always seemed genuinely puzzled by the hostile reaction to her life-style. She remarked to Sally Brompton of the *Sunday Express* on 16 January 1972: 'People know I have a sizeable house in the country and they confuse size with wealth. I don't mind telling you that the house I wanted was several thousand pounds more than the one we got. Shirley Williams came from a much better background than I did and she also had a nanny for her children but she was never accused of half the things that I am.'

The fact that Mrs Williams' domestic help – whatever form it took – never attracted the same oppobrium is undoubtedly because Mrs Williams never assumed that a silver spoons life was the norm. One celebrated remark by Mrs Thatcher provides a classic example of how to put up the backs of ordinary working people: 'When the children were young I always had an English nanny. I never had an *au pair* because I couldn't really have gone out and left them with an easy mind. I wouldn't have been quite certain whether the *au pair* could speak English or knew how to ring the hospital if anything happened.'

Yet, just as Mrs Thatcher misunderstood the reactions of ordinary people whose lives had not been touched by the luck and privileges she had enjoyed, so they did not understand her. Her cultivated accent and affluent life-style, passports to acceptance within the Tory Party, did not tell the whole story. She did not possess the self-confidence engendered by a middle-class background that both Mrs Williams and Mrs Castle possessed. One Conservative contemporary of Mrs Thatcher's, who also knew the Betts family in Bradford, recalled: 'I remember my father saying of Frank Betts – if only he had to employ people, he wouldn't say half what he does. Being a civil servant gives you a security that people in trade never have. You're always afraid and always worried that something will go financially wrong. This is one of the most formative influences in life. Margaret had that insecurity; so did her husband until he made his money. You never shake it off. Shirley Williams never had to fight as Margaret did, and neither did Barbara Castle.'

5   *Press and Prejudice*

WHEN Tessa Jowell, the deputy director of the pressure group Mind, was selected by Labour to fight the critical Ilford North by-election in 1978, the press chose to regard this as a sign that women were now getting fairer treatment when it came to selecting parliamentary candidates. It was pointed out that Ms Jowell had been chosen in preference to two very impressive male candidates – so all credit to the local party that had chosen her, and all credit to her. But any idea that her selection marked a new golden age for women candidates was rudely dispelled a few weeks later by the vicious press campaign waged against her. The first hint of what was to come was provided when the *Daily Mail* rang her home number in order to speak to her. The phone was answered by David Mills, who she later married and with whom she was living at the time. The reporter asked him who he was – to which he replied that he lived there. Later that evening Tessa was phoned up by another reporter and subjected to a long and circuitous questioning which had little to do with politics. Did she live on her own? No? Well, just whom did she live with then? Did she live with her father, perhaps? And by the way, who was Roger Jowell? Her ex-husband? Mmnn, I see.

In the next few days, a press campaign started which threw Tessa badly off balance and poisoned the whole election campaign. Under the headline 'Love Confessions of Labour's Tessa', the *Daily Mirror* on 16 January 1978 breathlessly announced: 'Labour candidate Mrs Tessa

Jowell tossed a bombshell into a crucial by-election last night. She announced: "I'm living with a man who is not my husband." ' Little did it matter, apparently, that Tessa was the candidate for the party that the *Mirror* supported. The promise of titillation and scandal provided by details of her private life obviously outweighed political sympathies.

The Tory popular press leapt upon the story with even more drooling enthusiasm. The *Daily Mail*, under the headline 'My Love Affair by Labour Girl', proclaimed on 26 January: 'A woman chosen by Labour to fight a crucial by-election yesterday dismissed her affair with a married man as "irrelevant". Divorcee Mrs Tessa Jowell said she had made no secret of her personal life either before or after her selection as candidate to defend a 778 majority in Ilford North. The 30 year old social worker is living with a fellow Labour member of Camden council, 34-year-old lawyer David Mills, who parted from his wife and three children in October 1976. Mrs Jowell's former husband, Roger, is an alderman on the same council and lives only a mile away from the couple. "I've absolutely nothing to be ashamed of. My private life is my own affair," she said. The chairman of Ilford North selection committee, Mr Roy Emmett, said: "We are electing an M.P., not the Archbishop of Canterbury." '

The story obviously had everything. Not only were both parties to the affair Labour politicians; both had been married before, and David Mills wasn't even divorced yet. And to cap it all, the former husband – by implication the wronged party – was living just down the road. In vain did Tessa state and re-state the obvious, that all of this was no one's business but her own and irrelevant to the campaign. The *Daily Express* on 25 January sanctimoniously announced, under the headline 'My Secret Lover, by Tessa': 'Pretty Mrs Tessa Jowell . . . admitted last night: "I'm living with a married man who is not my husband." Did the selection panel know of Mrs Jowell's domestic arrangement? Tessa, whose own marriage ended four months ago after a two year separation, said: "I told them I was divorced. Our relationship has nothing to do with the issues on which the by-election will be fought." '

It is hard to say what impact all this nonsense had on the by-election itself, which Labour eventually lost. Certainly there was at least some local reaction. David Mills, out canvassing for Tessa in Ilford, was told by one woman that she wasn't going to vote Labour because the candidate lived with some man. 'I am the man,' announced Mr Mills – and by all accounts the long conversation that then ensued persuaded this particular citizen that Tessa was the best candidate for the job.

No male candidate would have been subjected to the same kind of harassment. Male candidates have been separated or divorced or living with people, yet the scavengers of Fleet Street have left them alone. Women candidates face popular attitudes which dictate that their moral standards must be absolutely beyond reproach, an expectation that is not made of their male colleagues. Whether this is an attitude prevalent in the community and simply reflected by certain sections of the press, or whether it is an attitude foisted on to the community by a newspaper industry dominated by men, is not immediately clear. There is, self-evidently, a market for this kind of story: newspaper sales certainly do not slump whenever they appear. There are undoubtedly certain prejudices against women which are ripe for exploitation, prejudices which mean that women who choose to pursue careers rather than confine themselves to home and family are viewed with some disfavour. Women who choose careers that are regarded as male domains are viewed with even greater hostility. And if women choose to brave this disapproval and emerge into the public eye, then they are permitted no sexual peccadilloes; indiscretions which would be regarded indulgently, even admiringly, as being natural in men are condemned as wholly unnatural when practised by women.

Such prejudices are fully appreciated by 'family' newspapers, whose largely male staffs harbour similar attitudes to the ones that they know exist among their readers and which, they know, offer a lucrative source to be tapped. People love to be shocked, to be able to pass moral judgments on others, to measure their own behaviour by the profligacy of other people so that they can emerge reassured of their own unblemished moral rectitude. Prurience is an exploitable commodity, and deeply engrained assumptions about the behaviour of women mean that there is ample scope for the prurient when these assumptions are challenged.

In their treatment of women politicians and parliamentary candidates, however, newspapers have always been dominated by disapproving or blatantly hostile attitudes which appear to do more than merely echo the prejudices of the community; in some cases, the extreme hostility displayed by the press has seemed to reflect a male fear of being overtaken and dominated by an unstoppable army of women in Parliament. Such an attitude was most blatant in the early days of women's suffrage, when the idea of women in Parliament was very much a novelty. But although the idea is no longer novel, women politicians are still seen as somewhat freakish by virtue of their always tiny numbers. Correspondingly, attitudes in the press have not fundamentally changed. Outright hostility now wears a subtle overcoat under which women are patronised and demeaned. Newspapers talk approvingly of increases in the numbers of women candidates standing for Parliament, and note regretfully that the numbers actually winning seats are even being reduced from their previously risible levels. But these are platitudes uttered in deference to the social conventions which dictate lip-service to the notion of equality for women. When such newspapers call for more women M.P.s, they mean they would like to see, say, fifty or sixty women in Parliament. Were this to happen, they would no doubt announce that the age of equality had truly arrived. But real equality, in terms of Parliamentary representation, would mean at least 318 women M.P.s – or more than half the total number, since women outnumber men in the community. One can only imagine the thinly veiled horror that would greet such an event among the purveyors of liberal platitudes in the press.

Fifty years ago that horror was not even thinly veiled. The bitterly contested right of women to sit in Parliament was regarded by some commentators as the thin end of a wedge that would lead to a feminine dictatorship. The *Sunday Pictorial* in 1927 ran a headline: 'When Women Rule the World: Matriarchal state predicted for 1947', under which it warned: 'The little band of women sitting today at Westminster are but the single spies of the battalions to come.' As evidence of this cataclysmic reversal of the natural order, it informed its readers of the steady tendency of girls to refuse to undertake domestic responsibilities.

Even among those who did not necessarily believe in the imminence of a female takeover, there was overt and often vicious hostility, masquerading in part as a concern to uphold and develop to its full potential the unique value of women's contribution to society. A rather confused correspondent, A.A. Baumann, wrote in the London *Evening Standard* on 18 August 1931: 'I don't like women in Parliament... There must be of necessity many minds and much discussion of a decidedly coarse texture from which I think women ought to be sheltered... Will anyone be kind enough to tell me specifically how many female M.P.s have dulcified or raised the tone of debates or contributed any fresh or valuable information to the national interest? In other words, what have any of them said or done that could not have been said or done better by a man? Dr Johnson said that a woman making a speech was like a dog walking on its hind legs – the thing is not well done, but we are surprised that it is done at all. The rough truth of the doctor's saying lingers at the back of our heads and most women get elected, I believe, from a secret admiration that they are there at all. What a waste of precious material! Have we so many clever and accomplished women that we can afford to stick a conventional label on their heads and shut them up in poky little rooms waiting for the division bell?'

Women politicians were then, as they still are now, caught in a cleft stick. They were accused of being different from men and therefore suspect as politicians, of being emotional rather than logical, impulsive rather than considered, and so forth. Yet at the same time they were accused of being too much like their male colleagues, of not contributing a difference of approach and therefore failing to justify their presence in Parliament. One example of this attitude was provided in the *Daily Mirror* on 22 March 1934, when women were upbraided by the writer for failing to solve the problems of the world, particularly the dangers of chemical and bacteriological warfare: 'What are the women of this country thinking, planning and doing to prevent such a catastrophe? I can supply the answer in one word: nothing. Yet from their very numbers their political influence, not to mention their personal influence, ought to be paramount – and still they shirk the responsibility of constructive work in the cause of peace. Unfortunately, women in the mass never seem able to grasp abstract subjects. A vote was something personal, but the ideal of world peace fails to arouse feminine imagination. Therefore as far as women are concerned, mothers can continue to die in childbirth, or live in slums, or remain tied to insane husbands, and London be sown with gas bombs and cholera germs from the air in the next war. Women might do a great deal to prevent these unfortunate happenings if they liked, but the truth is that the majority are too idle-minded to bother.'

Most press comment on the issue of women politicians has been marked by hypocritical double standards, in which superficial objectivity and respect for women's abilities have gone hand in hand with swiping assaults based on sheer prejudice. Take, for example, this comment from the *Evening Standard* on 22 January 1935, after the Labour Party's national agent had bemoaned the low number of women parliamentary candidates. 'Mr Shepherd [the agent] says that a woman of ability is much to be preferred to a man who takes the job too easily.

That will be generally accepted. Given a man and a woman of equal ability, the choice in most cases, I believe, would go to the man. Candidates are chosen by local political bodies on which, generally speaking, men and women have equal representation. Experienced organisers say that women frown on women candidates. Men also prefer to be represented by their own sex. Many more women volunteer as candidates than are selected. Politicians think that women are handicapped as candidates. Their voices will not stand the strain of open air meetings; they are less adroit than men in answering difficult questions; they are inexpert with interrupters.'

The occasional accolades from the press were also spiked with acid. In 1939, J.B. Firth wrote in the *Daily Telegraph* that women had fallen in smoothly with the traditions of the House of Commons. 'They have not been self-assertive or – with rare exceptions – provocative. I would not say that they have yet produced any great "stars" but they have won many quiet triumphs in debate which have achieved generous recognition. It is, in fact, quite an exploded idea that women are only useful in Parliament in order to safeguard the interests of women and children. Since the Great War, in which women established their claim to the vote by their noble service and their unflinching endurance, the civic status of women has enormously improved and their economic position has kept an almost equal pace. Neither may satisfy the extreme advocates of feminism but the advance is remarkable and there is no sign of it becoming static.'

In fact, women's civic status is still inferior to that of men, their economic position is still far away from equality, and the advance is remarkable only in that it has failed to occur. The equivocations of this passage were scarcely surprising in view of the patronising offensiveness of another comment in the same paper seven years previously on 29 October 1932: 'I am surprised that we do not hear more of the women members of the House of Commons. Half a dozen of them at least are clever and able debaters. When Mrs Ward, the Conservative member for Cannock, asked a supplementary question the other day, her lucidity and economy of words were an example which many of the men M.P.s might envy. Some of the women are greatly superior to the majority of the men in this respect.' Dr Johnson's dog was clearly marching on its hind legs through the corridors of the *Telegraph* offices; the idea that women could be clever and lucid was obviously so surprising that the paper felt constrained to congratulate them for it.

When it came to the question of women holding Government office, the press was even more uneasy. The *Daily Telegraph* on 10 August 1945 actually had to invent a reason to explain to itself how Barbara Castle could have become Parliamentary Private Secretary to Sir Stafford Cripps, President of the Board of Trade. After all, this was not the typical women's job which women were expected to hold down, if they had to take office at all. Never mind – the *Telegraph* consoled itself by a reassuring swipe at the essential uselessness of women in such positions. 'A likely explanation is to be found in the fact that the Board of Trade is responsible both for the rationing of women's clothes and for the production of those utility garments about which many women complain. Mrs Castle will be able to keep Sir Stafford Cripps informed of the views of the women M.P.s on these subjects. There are few precedents for a woman as P.P.S. Their usefulness is limited by the fact that they are unable to retail to a Minister the back bench talk and the gossip of the smoking rooms. There are few Parliamentary fields now in which women still have not gained a foothold. Two still uninvaded are the law officers' department and the Whips' office. I predict that the latter will be the first of these to fall to feminine assault.' True enough – but there has yet to be a woman law officer, and the first woman whip was not appointed for twenty years after the *Telegraph*'s comments.

When the press was not describing women politicians in terms that would be more appropriate for a creeping fungus, it was busy parcelling them up into stereotypes from which they have still not escaped. The image of the woman as the bossy or nagging wife, the pecking hen, has always been the humorists' stock in trade, and political journalists, when searching for a joke, are no exception. The presence of women in Parliament has, indeed, been a gift to some of them, and this is a characteristic of both the popular and the serious press. The *Guardian*, in 1967, reported an incident that occurred when Kenneth Robinson, the Health Secretary, uttered some 'anti-feminist sentiments'. The report went on: 'There followed a loud "hear, hear" from Dr John Dunwoody on the benches behind him. This in turn was followed by an even louder thwack, the sound of Dunwoody's head being smitten by a rolled order paper wielded by Mrs Gwyneth Dunwoody sitting just behind.'

Women, especially in the Tory Party, were seen as fulfilling the overwhelmingly important function of wives, openers of fêtes and unpaid secretaries; unsurprisingly, the *Telegraph* writer, Winefride Jackson, wholeheartedly espoused this view. On 13 March 1958 she wrote an article on the usefulness of glamour among the wives of candidates. She wrote of one such paragon: 'She can type. She also goes around with an ever-ready pad of paper on which to take down additional notes for speeches as inspiration hits her husband driving through the countryside. The wives of today's young candidates have some pretty high standards with which to judge their own. On the whole, men are lucky.'

The logical culmination of such an attitude was that women should be interviewed by parliamentary selection panels in the constituencies – not in their own right as candidates, of course, but as attractive appendages to their husbands. A leader in the *Daily Telegraph* on 12 February 1971 approved of this procedure, which was then being carried out at Arundel and Shoreham. 'Who can doubt, however, the need for such examinations? Any M.P.'s efficiency can depend largely on the skill, tact and industry of his spouse. Let us be frank; even her appearance may turn out to be a political asset or a liability . . . The three Tory ladies at Arundel and Shoreham make no complaint about their forthcoming inquisitorial luncheon. That does them credit, and entitles each of them to an encouraging pat on the back as she moves into action.'

The overwhelming disadvantage from which women in Parliament have always suffered, encountered in all sections of the press, is that they have been ascribed certain characteristics as a group. That very stereotyping diminishes them, since it reinforces the impression that they are different, freakish; and the characteristics they have been ascribed are themselves less than flattering. The so-called feminine qualities of sympathy, intuition and compassion are thereby balanced out by a corresponding lack of logic, incisiveness and competence. When these qualities are discovered in an able woman Parliamentarian, they are therefore cause for comment; when they are discovered in a man, they may cause him to be the subject of flattering references but without the patronising condescension that marks such comments about his female colleagues.

Hence the *Sunday Times*, on 3 February 1952, commented on Florence Horsbrugh, then the Education Minister: 'To the sympathy and warm heart of a woman she adds a solid good sense and ability to get things done which is rarer in politicians of her sex.' The *Guardian*, on 21 December 1940, obviously thought that strong intellect was the prerogative of men. In a tribute to the work done by women M.P.s, it remarked of Eleanor Rathbone that intellectually she surpassed all the other women members: 'Her mind has a masculine solidity.' And in 1963 the same paper perpetuated some more stereotypes: 'Miss Mervyn Pike, the new Under-Secretary of State at the Home Office, has always been one of the quieter of the women at Westminster. She has never been handicapped by the vehemence often associated with women politicians but is generally thought of as competent, conscientious, a quiet dresser and good at her work.' While in 1967, it commented on Judith Hart: 'Barbara Castle may care to note that another woman Minister is looking devastatingly competent.'

With such praise, it might be thought, who needed detractors? Yet at the same time that the press was perpetuating such prejudices, it was complaining that women were not playing a full part in politics. *The Times* asked on 3 June 1957: 'But where after 38 years . . . is the woman member of Parliament who can speak with authority in the wider fields of foreign and commonwealth policies? Many women of both parties have considerable knowledge of colonial affairs which is respected by their male colleagues. But authority in these fields still eludes them. Are they being prevented by lack of opportunity or by not being given a voice? Or have they themselves not kept pace with the challenge of having achieved first objectives? Having done this, are they being slow to move on?'

In view of the handicaps suffered by women politicians through their presentation in the press, such questions seem colossal cheek. Ever since Nancy Astor took her seat in the House of Commons more than sixty years ago, the presence of women in Parliament has remained a constant source of fascination to the press. Their rarity value makes them a potent source of stories, but it seems that the only way for them to avoid hostile publicity is to keep their heads down and do nothing to attract any attention to themselves. Even natural characteristics like a particularly high voice or an attractive face are used time and again in the press as devices to entertain the reading public at the expense of the woman concerned. It is far worse if by her behaviour the woman M.P. deliberately draws attention to herself, as both Maureen Colquhoun and Helene Hayman found out to their cost.

Maureen Colquhoun was rash enough to declare publicly that she was a lesbian. She did so in order to bring home to the public that the ranks of public figures contained their fair share of homosexuals; she believed that until homosexuals declared their sexual inclinations, they would always remain a persecuted minority. She maintained that her lesbianism was the main reason why her constituency party in Northampton mounted a strenuous campaign to prevent her from being reselected as their parliamentary candidate. Whether or not it played a significant part in that episode, her declaration of lesbianism rebounded badly on her in the press. There was hardly a newspaper story about her after that which did not begin 'Maureen Colquhoun, the self-confessed lesbian M.P.' or with some similar rubric. One could argue that she had only herself to blame for this, since she had made a point, on several occasions, of mentioning this particular fact. But the mauling she received at the hands of journalists, who were clearly outraged and offended by the fact that she was a lesbian – and had had the effrontery to force this fact into the open – was vicious indeed. Any sexual indiscretion by a woman in public life is regarded as a tasty morsel for prurient appetites, but lesbianism in a married woman with three children totally outraged the sensibilities of these who proceeded to capitalise upon the disclosure.

The *Sunday Express*, for example, on 17 September 1978 suddenly adopted a role as the defender of the innocence of children in its moralising comments: 'Has she considered what the effects of flaunting her lesbianism might be on her three children? Does she imagine it helps them very much to have the whole world know that every night their elderly mum chases another elderly and equally unprepossessing lady round the bedroom? Ugh!' The last sentiment might well have been reserved as a comment on its own unpleasant and offensive observations. The most hypocritical comments were to be found in the *Daily Express* on 5 April of that year where Jean Rook, under the headline 'The Gay Lady is a Bore', felt justified in milking the story further under the guise of finding it all too boring to be even considered. Jean Rook was somewhat miffed to see that Maureen Colquhoun was proclaiming that she was a lesbian at the same time as insisting that her private life was her own affair. The contradictions of this were too much for the columnist to take. 'What is private about Ms Colquhoun's life?' she asked. 'For months she's gone on and on about it, often on telly. She's opened her heart and mouth, flung wide her bedroom door and all but shown us the colour of her and her friend's Hers and Hers toothbrushes. If Ms Colquhoun, at 49, has had a lovely, torrid change of love life, that's her business. I wish she'd stop trying to make it mine.' But though it was none of her business, this was quite evidently the very business Jean Rook was in. Scandal and sexual titillation are the stock-in-trade of gossip writers, as the offended M.P. pointed out in a reply to the article.

The fact that Ms Colquhoun had been attempting to make a protest about some of the hypocrisy of public life, and to remove some of the voyeurism that dogs public figures, had been lost sight of. By running her reply to the article, and inviting comments from readers – which considerably extended the impact of the original article – the *Express* gained the maximum sensational mileage out of the whole affair.

Helene Hayman encountered a similar barrage of often malevolent comment, although for quite different reasons, when she took her new-born son, Benjamin, into the House of Commons to feed him. She had to do this, she explained, because at a time when the minority Labour government was wobbling precariously on its legislative course, the party whips would not allow Mrs Hayman to be paired. Bringing the baby in and feeding him created a predictable press sensation, especially when the Government survived by a majority of one on its move to guillotine debate on nationalising the aircraft and shipbuilding industries. This provided ample opportunity to run large photographs of 'the baby that helped the Government to victory'. Less predictable were the sharp noises of disapproval, often from women columnists who chose to view the whole exercise as a publicity stunt by Mrs Hayman. One writer in the *Sunday People* wrote on 7 November 1978: 'I am alarmed that a woman intelligent enough to be an M.P. is apparently not bright enough or resourceful enough to organise her baby-rearing duties separately from her job. She certainly isn't doing women's rights any favours by trying to blackmail men that she'll unbutton her blouse and feed her child in Parliament. If, as Mrs Hayman screeches, "It's the most fantastic thing in the world to have a baby", then she should sit down quietly and enjoy it and not expect a job to fit in with her chosen pleasures.'

As if such comment was not bad enough, Mrs Hayman had to put up with a virtual siege by photographers at her London home. 'At one point, the photographers congregated outside the house and one even blocked my car door so that I had to stand still while he took a picture before I could get the carrycot out of the back of the car,' she told me. 'If you don't want to give up feeding your baby you have to accept that whatever you do is news.'

Nevertheless, upsetting as it undoubtedly is to have one's privacy invaded, there is a distinct ambivalence about this kind of relationship with the press. Clearly Mrs Hayman was distressed by the press siege of her home and by the subsequent sniping from newspaper columnists. But why had she announced her intention to take the baby to the House if she really wanted to shield her private life from the glare of publicity? Could it have been that she really had no objection to publicity over her intention to feed the baby at Westminster – provided it was sympathetic and the photographers kept their distance? Helene Hayman has always had a curious relationship with the press, from whose treatment she has both suffered and benefited simultaneously. All publicity is good publicity for a young M.P. trying to struggle up the greasy pole, but the kind of publicity she has received has invariably presented her as someone not to be taken seriously.

She has suffered from the crippling disadvantages of being not only young and female but attractive – a combination regarded by the press as a veritable licence to trivialise. Just as Maureen Colquhoun found it impossible to shake off the 'self-confessed lesbian' tag even in the most unlikely press reports, so Helene Hayman became 'young and attractive' in countless newspaper columns, which were often graced by a photograph. In 1976, speculation grew that the Prime Minister, Harold Wilson, was considering appointing Mrs Hayman to a Government post. The *Sunday Express* on 29 February 1976 suggested that he wanted to boost the ranks of women in his government. It went on: 'A current favourite is Mrs Helene Hayman, the winsome little filly who sits for Welwyn and Hatfield.' On 15 May 1975 the *Daily Express,* under the headline 'Helene could put glamour in Harold's big facelift', announced: 'There is growing talk . . . that a pretty young rabbit will pop out of Harold Wilson's hat next month. Giving Helene a junior job is the sort of job at which wily Wilson excels. She is female, she is young, she has only been an M.P. for seven months and no woman has ever been a minister so young. He reckons it would be bound to make headlines big enough to submerge for a moment the close-focus on cannibalism in the party.' So much for merit – although as an afterthought the writer did go on to praise Mrs Hayman's political virtues.

It is nevertheless possible for a woman M.P. to be attractive and dress well and still command the respect of the press for her intellectual and political abilities. Barbara Castle managed it; the press were mesmerised by her, mainly because of the force of her personality and the fact that she gave them the showmanship they craved. The fact that she had achieved office almost as soon as she entered Parliament, her considerable gift of oratory, and the fact that she made a spectacular success – at least in the days before the troubled period of *In Place of Strife* – of every job she was given, all contributed to their respect for her. David

Watt wrote in the *Financial Times* on 19 April 1969: 'Barbara Castle has that kind of star quality given only to a tiny handful of entertainers in any generation – and to almost no politician – that of making the crowd lean forward in their seats when she steps onto the stage. Another attribute of the star is that she must throw herself entirely on the mercy of the audience. Nothing must be held back. The tears, smiles, hopes, fears, loves, hates, must all be shared with the fans. And here again Barbara Castle has the necessary. She is a complex woman, but here again her complexities are all in the open. We can see that she is courageous, opportunistic, intelligent, self-deceiving, emotional, calculating, principled and ambitious. But we never know in each breathless instalment which quality or combination of qualities is going to win.'

Another reason for Mrs Castle's success with the press was that, as in every other sphere of her political life, she always took the bull of prejudice by the horns before it had a chance to gore her. An account in the *Guardian* by J.R.L. Anderson on 7 January 1966 of her press conference as Minister of Transport illustrates the point. 'In a bright red frock, and wearing a necklace of chunky old gold costume jewellery, Mrs Castle faced her first ordeal by press conference as Minister of Transport yesterday. With photographers' flashbulbs going off all round her, she made almost a film star's entrance to the Minister's rather drab conference room. "I want to give you a chance to have a look at this woman who can't even drive," she said demurely. Rare thing at a press conference, one or two people clapped her entrance and then simply stopped applauding in a slightly embarrassed fashion. But you wanted to applaud; Mrs Castle is a woman, she is Minister of Transport and she can't drive. Was she going to take to driving now? "No," she said, "and no for the sake of matrimonial harmony. One family, one car, means one husband, one car." One could sense the approval of every man in the room; the women there bristled slightly. Splendid strike in the sex war (but on whose side?).'

If that inaugural press conference had occurred ten years later, Mrs Castle would not have made that last remark, since it would have been quite out of tune with the social expectations of the times. But she used it then as a device to get the men of the press on to her side; in that cause, she was prepared to enlist traditional prejudices against women if they would help her – and she was successful.

Nevertheless, even she did not escape the overriding fascination of the press with every detail of the appearance of the woman M.P. Paul

Johnson, for instance, wrote in the *Daily Mirror* on 26 July 1968 about the First Secretary of State: 'Her bright red hair is always in place. She is clean, scented, carefully made up. Her clothes are bandbox fresh. She spends a great deal of money on them and it is worth every penny.' And the *Guardian* delightedly reported on 5 July 1960, on the occasion of Mrs Castle's arrival in the Commons attired in a white hat: 'When male members of Parliament on both sides of the House are so conservative in dress, the appearance of Mrs Barbara Castle at Question Time has come to be the sartorial moment of every parliamentary day. Over the years, her wardrobe has in turn surprised and delighted her colleagues and as with royalty it has come to be a point of principle that Mrs Castle must not appear more than a few times in any outfit, however smart.' If such really were the preoccupations of M.P.s, one can only conclude it is small wonder that the difficulties of the country they governed became so severe.

The press obsession with their clothes has affected almost all women M.P.s. Patricia Hornsby-Smith's first day as Joint Parliamentary Secretary at the Ministry of Health in 1951 was marked by the *Guardian* on 29 November in this way: 'She turned up at the Ministry of Health's brand new HQ in Savile Row looking very much the brand new parliamentary secretary. Miss Hornsby-Smith wore a black suit with a silver ornament in the lapel and a neat white blouse.' Winefride Jackson in the *Daily Telegraph* asked Patricia Hornsby-Smith and Priscilla Tweedsmuir what they planned to wear on the first day of the new Parliament in 1950. 'Black, of course!' they replied. 'We want to look as though we mean business!' Not much hope of that, with such reported comments.

Mervyn Pike, when she won Melton Mowbray in 1956, earned one of the most backhanded compliments of all. 'Jaded Friday members were agreeably impressed by her trim composure. Unlike some women M.P.s, she is much more prepossessing in person than in her photographs. Her smart maroon suit set off a matronly figure and she managed the stately pavane to the table without a fault.' Even Shirley Williams, blue-stockinged heroine of the press, could not escape this sort of demeaning newspaper coverage. The *Daily Mirror* on 30 December 1970 burbled: 'Shirley is solid, half girl, half matron; she has clothes that keep her warm, a hair-do that sometimes looks like a home perm and an adorable waddling walk like that of a barefoot goosegirl. I'm always reminded of St Joan. Britain's first woman Prime Minister? I doubt it; and so would she.' So would anyone, after such a presentation; there is no place for barefoot goosegirls in Number 10.

The person who has suffered most strikingly from such trivialisation, however, is Margaret Thatcher – most strikingly because of the often absurd terms in which she has been described in the past, and the contrast between this image and that of a Prime Minister. Journalists have appreciated the quality of her intellect and the fine performances she occasionally puts on in the House; but they just haven't been able to reconcile this with the other, physical aspects of her. An amusing specimen of this type of reporting was provided by *The Times* on 6 May 1966. John Diamond, Chief Secretary to the Treasury, had been attacked during the Budget debate by Mrs Thatcher, then the opposition front bench spokesman. *The Times*'s Parliamentary Correspondent described the event: 'With her blonde curls a constant bobbing reminder of the prospective increase in hairdressing charges she attacked the whole structure of the tax with incisive feminine logic. Mr Diamond and Mr Callaghan at his side soon found themselves assaulted with every female weapon short of a rolling pin. Mrs Thatcher had certainly been doing her homework. She had read, or so she said, every Budget speech and every Finance Bill since 1946. The Commons received this news with little short of awe . . . By this time she was in full stride, her impeccable accent beginning to hammer on Labour ears like some devilish Roedean water torture. In her eyes, the Chancellor had been no friend to women, particularly married women and widows who had to go out to work. They were forced, she said, to employ someone to look after their children. Now, just to add to their burden, they would have to pay another 12s. 6d. a week for the privilege. Mr Diamond jumped to his feet. At last he saw a chance to get his own back. "The Hon. Lady must know," he said, "that this is a tax on employers." Mrs Thatcher turned on her most feline smile. "Precisely," she replied. "These women are employers. Clearly the Front Bench have not even thought of this. Perhaps now they will do something about it." '

As an example of prejudiced journalism, this passage has just about everything. Mrs Thatcher obviously trounced the hapless Mr Diamond by having done her homework and by being quick on her Parliamentary feet. (He also happened to reveal his own narrow assumptions about the role of women in to the bargain.) If Mrs Thatcher had been a man, the *Times* reporter would probably have related the incident in a straightforwardly admiring way, pointing out the skill with which one parliamentarian scored a point over another. But instead he sought to turn it into a humorous anecdote – Dr Johnson's dog at large again – and to belittle Mrs Thatcher's achievement by using stereotyped images: the rolling pin, the hairdressing charges, the nagging voice and the feline smile.

From her earliest days in politics, Margaret Thatcher has been represented by journalists as a kind of Salome of the suburbs; the image bestowed upon her has been an absurd mixture of garden fête manners and the kind of deadly temptress behaviour that would be more suited to a bad film. It is an image that has been conveyed by women journalists as well as men. For example, Irene Hanstatter wrote in the *Daily Telegraph* on 3 February 1950 about the various women trying to get into Parliament, among whom was the young Margaret Roberts. The article said of the future Prime Minister: 'She is a good pianist, loves colourful, well-cut clothes and cooking. She is an effective elocutionist. She forgets party politics and her eyes gleam as she remembers how she first met Dartford's Labour candidate, Mr Norman Dodds M.P. It was at a ball. Margaret wore black velvet and pearls. She danced an exhibition tango with Dodds while the rest of the company looked on. The tune she requested was "Jealousy".' Of the women candidates, Irene Hanstatter concluded: 'One thing each has in common. They will each fight the election battle on an equal basis with men.'

The press was simply unable to accept Mrs Thatcher on the basis of her merits and weaknesses as they would any male politician. Even her debut on the floor of the House of Commons, universally praised as being one of the most effective performances ever witnessed by her contemporaries, fell victim to trivialisation. The *Daily Telegraph* on 6 February 1960 enthused: 'As a maiden speech it has not been and is unlikely to be excelled by any of her contemporaries new to the 1959 Parliament. As a 30-minute exposition without a note of a controversial and complex Bill it was of front bench quality . . . To her intellectual and forensic abilities she added yesterday a new frock and not merely charm but an uncanny instinct for the mood of the House which some members take years to acquire – and many never acquire at all.'

On 26 October 1969, after she had become Opposition education spokesman, a *Sunday Telegraph* profile writer, Ivan Rowan, said: 'Mrs Thatcher is a very pretty woman in a soft suburban way with a nice mouth and nice teeth and large round dolly eyes like a candy box tied off with two shiny bows of blue ribbon.' Even as her political stature grew, more newspaper column inches were devoted to examining her appearance than her policies. The *Sunday Times* commented on 16 September 1973: 'She has lively blonde hair, though it is still a bit on the soft side, enviable pink and white skin, pretty hands, extremely shapely legs and her navy-blue suit was flattering, well-made and modern.'

Those very newspapers which later chose to view her as the saviour of Britain continued to discuss her personal appearance in the thick of the Conservative leadership crisis. The *Daily Mail* told its readers in January 1975 that Mrs Thatcher shopped at Jaeger and Duttons for her clothes. 'She wears tan tights which she gets from Marks and Spencer. Her hats? Pity to spoil a legend, but she hasn't bought a new one for two years and often wore them only because she regarded them as an easy way to camouflage untidy hair she didn't have time to do.'

Yet, as we have seen, Mrs Thatcher has encouraged journalists to think of her as a typical housewife, an image they are only too happy to present. Colin Dunne, writing in the *Daily Mirror*, summed up this somewhat baffling image on 3 February 1975: 'Margaret Thatcher had all her chores neatly lined up at the weekend. First there was the kitchen to tidy. Then the bathroom, a dash around with the duster and on to the shopping and the laundry. And after that she had to tidy up the Tory party, polish off Ted Heath and give Britain a good spring cleaning. With Margaret Thatcher it's sometimes a bit hard to tell whether she wants to be Prime Minister or housewife of the year.'

Coverage of her in the 1979 election campaign was hardly any better – although here again Mrs Thatcher seemed happy to help put across an image that would have been better suited to a women's magazine than to reports of the most critical general election since the war. Although the interviews she gave to the press during this time were extremely rare, she agreed to be interviewed on 16 March by Katharine Hadley of the *Sun* on 'My face, My Figure, My Diet'. In this, we learned how she inconspicuously restricted her diet, how she looked after her skin, and where she bought her clothes. It was not that the reporter was distorting with trivia a serious interview given in good faith; the woman who was to become Prime Minister within a few weeks entered into the spirit of the thing with gusto. '"Now look," she pointed to her neck. "This is the worst bit on a woman of my age. If you lower your chin while giving a speech then you look all double chins. I have to remember to keep my head up all the time."'

If she was willing to bring herself down to this level, she could hardly complain about the sort of coverage she got. On the very day after she became Prime Minister, the *Daily Mail* asked: 'So, after all this tension, pressure and strain, how does she still manage to look so radiant? Every woman knows the answer to that. Success at what you have chosen to succeed in makes the skin shine and the eyes bright.'

Even an apparently serious attempt to interview her on her policies, by George Gale of the *Daily Express* on 12 April 1979, degenerated into absurdity when Mrs Thatcher eagerly launched into a discussion of what to do with minced beef. Her much photographed pose with a broom, made on one of her publicity-seeking factory tours, provided a stereotyped image as ammunition for her opponents on the *Daily Mirror*. A front page comment by the paper's political editor appeared on 2 May 1979 next to such a photograph under the headline: 'What would YOUR life be like under Mrs Thatcher's broomstick?' conjuring up the image of both housewife and witch. And Ann Morrow in the *Daily Telegraph* treated voters to the following gem of useless information on 23 April: 'Today Mrs Thatcher's hair is all one length and a shade darker. Every Sunday her hairdresser, the retiring, soft-spoken "John", goes to her house in Chelsea at 9 a.m. and sets it for the week. Before the election campaign got under way, Mrs Thatcher used to dash to the salon in South Kensington and sit under the dryer surrounded by other clients such as Antonia Fraser, Anna Massey, Beryl Grey and the Countess of Rosebery.'

All the press agreed that Mrs Thatcher's sex and personality were election issues, but the two became inseparably intertwined. Commentators fell over themselves in their eagerness to point out that it was not Mrs Thatcher's sex to which they objected but her personality. It wasn't that she was a woman, more the type of woman she was. In some cases, the distinction was probably truthfully drawn, but this was by no means universal; sometimes critical discussion of her personality barely masked the underlying prejudice against women.

George Gale, however, made the distinction. Writing in the *Spectator* during the election campaign, he said that the fact that she was a woman was very much an issue, whether she liked it or not. His prejudices then displayed themselves almost immediately: 'I might here add that she is very much a female female. She is in no manner an imitation man who in her imitating proclaims the inferiority of her sex . . . she is less the reasoning and intellectual animal and more the passionate one than she affects . . . Her instincts are female and maternal. Her face mirrors her emotions, except when she is seeing to it that it doesn't. In short, she is a woman first and politician second.'

Partly because of Mrs Thatcher, the press paid more attention to women during the 1979 election campaign than it had ever done before – yet the treatment was just as patronising and trivial. For this the press was not entirely to blame. Mr Callaghan, for example, shamelessly used young and attractive women candidates at his press conferences to boost flagging interest. On one such occasion, he was flanked by Mrs Patricia Hollis, M.A., D.Phil., a university lecturer, and Mrs Anne Davis, B.A., a former teacher. These highly educated politicians were wheeled in because the theme of that morning's press conference was to be the family; as a result they were reduced to talking about the cost of children's shoes and the necessity of good bus services for women. But such lapses cannot excuse the more general attitudes prevalent in the newspaper coverage. In the *Daily Telegraph*'s focus on the Welwyn and Hatfield constituency, the paper plumped for the hairstyle of the Labour candidate, Helene Hayman, as the most interesting issue. Under two large photographs revealing that Mrs Hayman had cut her long hair short, the report revealed that her previous 'glamour-girl' image was now felt to be inappropriate. And in the *Daily Mail*, Lynda Lee-Potter's comments were not improved by her awareness of the image she was putting forward: 'At the risk of being justifiably accused of trivialising an election which will rule our lives for three weeks and our future for five years, could I point out that women candidates will have a marginally greater chance of success if they have large bosoms and can act?' The apparent justification for this extraordinary statement was that five of the women standing for election or re-election had once aspired to a career on the stage.

Yet alongside all the patronising comments and jokes about the women standing for Parliament at that election, newspapers constantly reminded their readers that women were more important than ever before; their mass vote would decide the outcome of the election, and if they all welcomed the prospect of a woman becoming Prime Minister the Conservatives would be home and dry. The *Daily Mirror*, by the side of a photograph of a mother and child, declared across its front page: 'Women Care! That's why their vote is so vital.' It had recognised the danger that women might identify with Mrs Thatcher as a woman and vote Tory as a result, and so attempted to counter-attack by emphasising that it was always the women of the country who had to cope on a daily basis with the failures of Government policy, and that Tory policies were bound to fail.

How far are people influenced by the treatment given to women politicians by the press? Many feel that they are far more influenced by what they see on television, which was why it was so important for Mrs Thatcher to be seen doing ordinary things (albeit in an extraordinary way) in her nightly appearances on the small screen. It is also felt that readers are only marginally influenced by the attitudes and prejudices displayed in their newspapers. Were this not the case, the argument runs, the Labour Party would never have won a general election, since the overwhelming majority of newspapers support the Conservatives. We return, inevitably, to the chicken and egg argument over whether newspapers lead or simply reflect public opinion; the truth probably lies somewhere between the two. Prejudices and out-dated assumptions about women in public life undoubtedly do still pose some disadvantage to women in national politics. Press coverage reinforces those prejudices and makes it harder for women politicians to establish themselves in the public mind as serious contenders for the job of governing the country, on an equal basis with men. If the press adopted a straighter approach towards women politicians, then some of the barriers in society might be broken down more quickly. Despite this, Mrs Thatcher, who has suffered more than most from belittling press coverage, brushed that disadvantage aside to gain the highest political office of all. Her particular success even leads one to wonder whether, in her case, the manipulators of popular prejudices were themselves manipulated by an even more cynical and professional mind.

6 The Back-Door Politicians

ONE of the women life peers whom I interviewed in a deserted House of Lords bar told me she had something she particularly wanted to say before anyone else came in. 'I don't want anyone to hear me say this,' she said quietly, 'but some of us are rather disturbed by the fact that some women have been given peerages on account of their husbands. We feel that we should come here because of our own experience in public life and not because we happened to marry somebody.'

One could see what she meant – although in the circumstances of the House of Lords it did seem a rather peculiar thing to say. One could sympathise with her in her view of the battle to allow women to become life peers at all, a battle that was only won in 1958. In the debate on the Bill that enabled women to be given peerages, Lord Glasgow said: 'The main point is that many of us do not want women in this House. We do not want to sit beside them on these benches nor do we want to meet them in the library . . . We do not want it to become a House of Lords and Ladies. This is about the only place left in the kingdom where men can meet without women. For heaven's sake, let us keep it like that!' Lord Glasgow's sentiments did not, however, carry the day and in 1958 the first four women life peers took their seats in the House of Lords: Stella, Marchioness of Reading, Dame Katherine Elliot, Barbara Wootton and Baroness Ravensdale, who already held the title.

In view of the prejudiced hostility it aroused, the creation of women life peers could be seen as a long overdue extension of the right that had been granted to women in 1918 to sit in the House of Commons. After all, if there was a second chamber it was clearly nonsensical to deny to women the opportunity to sit in it as peers in their own right. And if it had taken a further forty years after Nancy Astor took her seat in the Commons before the first women were allowed to do the same in the Lords, it was hardly surprising that some women peers should now be disturbed that merit appeared to have given way to a kind of nepotism.

But such an objection *was* peculiar in view of the raison d'étre of the House of Lords itself. The concept of equal rights for women, not least in the political arena, is based on principles of justice and equality: every citizen should enjoy full democratic rights, regardless of sex. Women as well as men should have the right to participate in the running of the country and to that end should be able to play a full part, based on their merits, in the democratic process of selection and election. But the House of Lords is itself an anachronism within this system. Its composition is not based on concepts of justice and equality but on hereditary privilege and political patronage. Its members are not elected and are answerable to no one, yet they have political power and a part to play in the process of government. Some are in this position by reason of their birth, others are awarded a peerage as a favour bestowed upon them by the Prime Minister of the day. Though some peers have undoubtedly led lives of virtue and industry and civic worth, their place in the upper chamber of Parliament is not bestowed upon them by a grateful public which has recognised their worth and decided that it wants to be governed by such outstanding citizens. Life peerages are the fief of powerful politicians who may bestow them out of gratitude, friendship, respect – or a desire to boost the numbers of people sympathetic to their own political party, whose support is necessary to enable that party's legislation to get through the House of Lords.

This point was not missed in 1958 by some Labour women who were more concerned about the undemocratic nature of the House of Lords than the right of women to play a part in it. Most notable among these women was Jennie Lee, then an outstanding politician of the left. She referred to the Life Peerages Bill, which allowed women to be created life peers, as 'this dishonest, furtive Bill, this Bill which insolently leaves out of account those of us who do not believe in the House of Lords at all'. (In the light of these impassioned remarks, it is perhaps somewhat surprising that Jennie Lee accepted a peerage herself in 1970, as the Rt.

Hon. Baroness Lee of Asheridge.)

In view of the composition and constitutional significance of the House of Lords, it would seem rather irrelevant to cavil at those women who have been created peers as a mark of respect to their husbands. It is more interesting to consider as a group those women who have accepted peerages – and have even gone on to hold Government office – but who were never M.P.s themselves. A few women peers once sat in the House of Commons, and moved into the Lords in a progression as smooth as that from school to university. But for the vast majority, their only means of entry into national politics was through the back door provided by the House of Lords. A number of them had been married to men who had had distinguished political careers, but had had no direct experience of politics themselves. Some had tried unsuccessfully to become M.P.s; others had never entertained any desire to go into the House of Commons. Are the women in this last group true political animals; and if they are why did they never aspire to the Commons? Why did those who wanted to be M.P.s meet with no success? And did the political wives really yearn all the time for political careers of their own?

I spoke to nine women peers who had never been M.P.s. Among them were three who had made their careers in local government, one academic, one former civil servant, one party boss, two erstwhile political wives and one who had made her name as a political secretary. Only a few of them had ever wanted to become M.P.s, although all were women of outstanding intelligence and character and most had clearly always been interested in politics. One is now a Government Minister; a second is now a member of the European Parliament; and five of the others have held some Government office in the past.

Three women who had wanted to become M.P.s all came from very different backgrounds. Two of them, however, Lady Stedman and Lady Llewelyn-Davies, had been profoundly influenced by the Depression when they were young women. Lady Stedman, who was a Minister of State at the Department of the Environment in the last Callaghan administration, told me that she was virtually born into the Labour movement. Both her parents were active in local politics; her father, an iron moulder in Peterborough, was an active trade unionist and her mother worked with the women's section of the local Labour Party. As a child, the young Phyllis Adams, as she then was, often found herself dragooned into helping out at election time. Her political consciousness developed while she was still at the local grammar school, for at fourteen years old she became an active member of the Labour League of Youth. When she left school, she worked as a librarian in Peterborough until the war, and during that time she was sent as a delegate from the local Labour party women's section to the annual National Labour Women's Conference. During that conference, held in Wales, she saw things that were to leave an indelible impression upon her.

'During that time, we travelled for a day through the Rhondda Valley at the height of the Depression,' she recalled. 'That was very terrible. It had a tremendous effect upon me about what unemployment actually meant and what hard times were, and what should be done about them. As a result, I maintained an interest in the party throughout the years. I went into the fire service during the war, and when I came out I was very anxious that we should fight every county council seat in the 1946 election.'

Lady Llewelyn-Davies, who was Chief Whip in the Lords during the last Labour government, came from a quite different background. Her family was wealthy and strongly Conservative, interested in politics but not active politically; her father was a man of strong character who disapproved of further education for women. Notwithstanding this environment, Lady Llewelyn-Davies soon established herself as a person of even stronger character than her father, for at about twelve years old she became interested in politics – and, from her family's point of view, her politics were of the wrong kind. For she was brought up on Merseyside, a distressed and distressing area during the Depression; she saw that conditions were even worse in Wales, and the sights she saw during these years turned her into a socialist. 'My family reacted very badly when I became a socialist,' she told me. 'They didn't mind so much when I was at school, where I stood as a Labour candidate in a mock election and got three votes out of 340 – they didn't mind that, but my father was very upset when I became a Labour candidate. He said he didn't want a Bessie Braddock in the family. Nevertheless, when he died, I found he had collected a great pile of press cuttings about me. What made me think I must go into Parliament was that I couldn't believe that the system that produced the Depression was the right one.'

She joined the Labour League of Youth and, despite her father's opposition to further education for women, went up to Girton College, Cambridge, to read English. The civil war in Spain was the great issue of that time which absorbed her, as it did most politically interested undergraduates, and she also ran a workers' theatre group. When she came down, she worked as a research secretary for Philip Noel-Baker, then Labour M.P. for Derby, later to become a minister, with whom she was to work for a number of years.

The third member of this trio of women is Lady Young, now Minister of State at the Department of Education. Her father was an Oxford don who also had a seat on Oxford City Council as an Independent. Both parents took an active, intelligent interest in politics but their involvement stretched no further than the seat on the Council. Politics were a topic of family discussion; one of Lady Young's first memories was of her father speaking out against the Munich agreement of 1938. She herself read politics, philosophy and economics at Oxford; although she took no active part in undergraduate politics, she thought that the Labour Government was not running the country well, so she joined the Young Conservatives when she came down. 'I realised then that it was absolutely fascinating,' she recalled. 'A whole new world had opened up. I realised that this was something that needed to be taken very seriously. It draws you in; it's like a disease.'

In 1946 this 'disease' had led Lady Stedman to take on, at a few weeks' notice, the task of fighting an apparently quite unwinnable County Council seat based on a poor area near Peterborough cathedral. The 28-year-old undertook the task simply to keep the Labour Party flag flying, but she found herself propelled into local government by a ten-vote victory. Her husband, who was on the city council, inadvertently almost cost his wife her political career. Her seat had been won on the strength of the votes from the slums behind the cathedral, but when her husband demolished the slums and rehoused the inhabitants elsewhere Lady Stedman found that her constituency had been demolished as well and she lost her seat three years after being elected. It was, however, no more than a temporary setback; before long she was returned to the county council, where she sat until she went to the House of Lords. When she was elected, the Labour Party were in the minority on the Council, but because they were within three votes of a majority they were an effective group. Lady Stedman soon made her mark, but she was viewed, she remembers, as something of an oddity. 'Because most of my electors were in the very poor part of the city I wanted to go on to the social services committee, but I was told by some of my colleagues that they didn't think it was right for me to go on to it because it would mean I would be dealing with the seamy side of life. I did get on to it, but there was in-built opposition. I just got on and did the job.' She eventually became vice-chairman of the Council, having chaired its fire services committee where, armed with expertise from her war years, she reckoned she could probably run rings round the other members. She was also heavily involved in the National Labour Women's Committee, but was still able to combine her political activities with helping to run the family's rose-growing and landscape gardening business.

Her one attempt to enter Parliament nearly ended in disaster. She was invited by Anthony Greenwood, then president of the Hampstead Labour Party, to stand for selection as the party's Parliamentary candidate. 'I'd known him from my League of Youth days, when he was a bright boy,' she recalled. It was a hopeless seat for Labour, with a 32,000 Conservative majority, and Lady Stedman was selected to fight it. She provides a mischievous explanation for her success: 'I got it because I said I didn't know anything about foreign policy, and as Hampstead was full of Foreign Secretaries-to-be, there was no opposition to me!' But Lady Stedman did not treat the seat as hopeless; she attacked the task as if Hampstead were a winnable marginal, and eventually her health gave way under the strain. 'I was coming down to London for a week at a time, in between running a home in Peterborough and county council business, and I just cracked up. The doctor gave me an ultimatum, that I had to decide between local government and fighting the London seat.'

She settled for local government, her aspirations, such as they were, to enter national politics having been snuffed out by the Hampstead experience. Then in 1974 she received a letter from the Prime Minister, Harold Wilson, telling her that he was putting her name forward for a peerage. 'The letter came on a Saturday morning with a note from his private secretary saying the announcement was to be made the following Wednesday and so I was to let him know before then if I had any objections. I spent a sleepless night wondering whether to accept it or not. I thought it would take me away from local politics, and I wasn't sure if I wanted to get involved in Parliament. I didn't know how much time it would take up, and I don't like taking things on if I can't do them. In the end I decided to accept, because I thought that someone obviously wanted me to do the work.'

Lady Llewelyn-Davies was able to observe national political life from the close yet detached perspective of her position as a civil servant, which she held for about twelve years and which took her into the Transport Ministry and the Foreign Office. She recalls that she was never aware of any prejudice towards her on the grounds that she was a woman while she was at Transport, but attitudes at the Foreign Office were 'amazing'. 'On one occasion, I was sitting outside the Minister's room at the F.O. while his P.P.S. was in with him. The P.P.S. came out and remarked, "There's still no one here", even though I was right there sitting outside the room. At diplomatic dinners you were expected to go out of the room with the wives – and you still do if you're not careful. I went to Mexico three years ago instead of the Lord Privy Seal as the representative of the Queen at the inauguration of the new president. Even then, at the dinner we gave at the British embassy, our ambassador said that I could remain in the room after dinner but only as a great break from precedent.'

She left the civil service because she decided that she wanted to try her hand at deciding policies rather than administering them. She made three attempts to become an M.P., fighting Enoch Powell at Wolverhampton and then fighting Wandsworth Central twice. In Wolverhampton, the selection committee consisted entirely of men, who made no remark about the fact that she was a woman – but she says she is sure that they selected her with some reluctance. 'It was rather daring of them; they thought I might have to overcome some prejudice among the voters, and some people thought my sex was a disadvantage. In Wandsworth, I had some hostile questioning from the selection committee – such as questions about whether I was neglecting my children. In fact, I fought one election at Wandsworth while I was still feeding my second child, but I didn't tell them that.'

She was not particularly disappointed when she failed to get elected. 'The House itself didn't hold a lot of glamour and mystery for me,' she admitted. 'I knew a great deal about the Commons – I'd been in it as a civil servant through the most exciting times. I became secretary of the Labour Party Candidates' Association and tried to get conditions improved for all candidates and it was all marvellous fun. I had my youngest child when I was 43, and then went into an Africa educational trust, and by then I didn't really want to be an M.P. any more. Women in the Commons when I was observing them were superb – but the times are different now, a lot of the battles have been won. And there's no question that if you are a conscientious mother, life in the Commons can be terribly difficult, especially with a hung Parliament. If I were an M.P. and my children were ill, I'd probably tell the whips to go to hell!' She saw the peerage, when it was offered to her, as a way of pursuing her interest in politics without the strain. 'I disapproved of titles, but I realised it would mean I would be able to do politics at a less gruelling speed,' she said.

Like Lady Stedman, Lady Young also made her political career in local government – but unlike Lady Stedman or Lady Llewelyn-Davies, she badly wanted to become an M.P. and seems now to be rather resentful that she was denied the opportunity. She was elected on to Oxford Council in 1957 when she had two young children – a fact, she remembers, that raised quite a few eyebrows, since it was very unusual for women to go into local government if they had young children. After ten years as a councillor, she became leader of the Conservative group and, perhaps inevitably, was asked by the party if she would consider standing for Parliament. 'I had thought about it, and it was something I would very much like to have done,' she told me. 'I was on the party's official list of candidates, and said I would do it if I could get a seat near Oxford. The practical difficulties of having three children at home in Oxford and a constituency in, say, Yorkshire were such that I could not have done it. One factor is money; if you have no private means, then what you can do is limited. I often advise girls who want to go into politics to marry a man who works in London. Once you're an M.P. you've got to have somewhere to live in London, tie up your domestic arrangements properly, have your own car.'

But it wasn't just these practical difficulties that prevented her from becoming an M.P.; she is convinced that part of the difficulty was that she was a woman, and an intellectual woman at that. She tried for a seat near Birmingham but was not selected. 'It was partly because I was a woman,' she said. 'There is tremendous prejudice against women, and not just from men but from other women as well. Sometimes it comes from women who have not themselves done a job and are slightly jealous. And in our party, there's a certain amount of prejudice against what are regarded as intellectual women.' She was always very conscious of discrimination against women, and related an incident to illustrate this which occurred when she was chairman of Oxford's education committee. 'I insisted that women should be interviewed for jobs as heads of schools. One headmaster was very prejudiced against women and resisted me greatly. It was a mixed school, but he wouldn't have a woman as his deputy; he insisted that if a woman were appointed she should be the third mistress, and responsible for needlework. It was true that very few women actually applied for the job of deputy, but I made him interview three women for it.'

In view of this, it is hardly surprising that she chose to use the Women's National Advisory Committee of the party as her way into national politics, a body of which she eventually became chairman. 'It's a very good way up the ladder for women in the party,' she commented. 'It means anyone can join the party and go straight up. There's nothing to stop her; it's an internal party affair, and it means she can get to an important party position.'

After the Birmingham episode, she was preparing to try a number of other seats but she was then offered a life peerage. 'It was like a bolt from the blue,' she said. 'I had written to Ted Heath about something completely different and this came back instead. I thought it would be silly not to accept.' Within a year she had become a Baroness-in-Waiting (in other words a junior whip in the Lords), the first woman Conservative to achieve the position; a year later she was made a junior minister in the Department of the Environment. After Margaret Thatcher became leader of the party, she appointed Lady Young as the party's deputy chairman, the first time that position had been filled by a woman. It was a post of considerable importance in Conservative Party politics, since it made her responsible for the whole administration: pensions, salaries, budgets and so on. Even before the 1979 election, which brought her into office again, this time at Education, she had become respected as Mrs Thatcher's *eminence grise*; already, the myths were beginning to swirl about her. Party workers shook their heads in admiration at the way she had apparently 'shouldered' her way into the deputy chairmanship of the party, and spoke of the influence she had over Mrs Thatcher. The friendship between the two is undoubtedly cemented by the fact that each regards herself as an 'intellectual' woman – that is, a woman with a better brain and education than most male party members expect from their women colleagues – and has therefore suffered in the past from the stigma associated with this characteristic.

Through the party organisation and her place in the House of Lords Lady Young has penetrated the machinery of government as effectively as if she had succeeded in her attempt to become an M.P. Now that she is a Minister again, no doubt she is putting into practice her outlook on political life: 'To succeed in politics you've got to have good health and a natural philosophy. Politicians are either in the heights of elation or the depths of depression – and you've also got to have the temperament not to have a nervous breakdown.'

Lady Llewelyn-Davies could also lay claim to being an 'intellectual' woman, but she managed to avoid antagonising her male colleagues. They would often say to her that she was really extremely clever – because she made sure that she never made them feel that she *was* clever. She was obviously rushed off her feet as Chief Whip in the Lords, despite her initial hopes that a peerage would remove the strenuousness from politics for her. She arranged all the debates and business management in the House, and often had to work until well past midnight. 'I've never worked so hard in my life,' she remarked to me. (Among the peers whom she had to marshal was her husband, who was created a life peer four years before his wife.) Apart from the routine business of the Lords, she also enjoyed the rank of Captain of the Honourable Corps of Gentlemen-at-Arms, a post which goes with that of Chief Whip. This charming anachronism became even more absurd when Lady Llewelyn-Davies became the first woman to be appointed to it. 'I'm on duty whenever the Queen has a state visit, and have to inspect my troops with their twelve-foot axes. The poor gentlemen nearly fainted when I was appointed,' she told me in considerable amusement.

It is a curious fact that the House of Lords, which one might have expected to be the last bastion of reactionary attitudes, has a better record for treating its women as equals than its sister chamber. Every woman to whom I spoke – some of them embattled feminists of many years' standing – emphasised this point. Lady Llewelyn-Davies was only its first woman Chief Whip, it is true, but the Commons has yet to achieve even that breakthrough. If a woman peer wants to hold some kind of office, she will have far less difficulty than a woman M.P. Why should this be so?

A number of explanations were proffered to me. For a start, there are none of the pressures that beset M.P.s who are ambitious to get on and make their mark and who have to elbow each other out of the way if they want to start clambering up the greasy pole of power. Peers arrive in the Lords with their reputations already made. They have all achieved something before arriving; they have lived lives spent doing good works, making money, chairing magistrates' benches, presiding over boards of governors. They are mainly middle-aged or elderly; they haven't fought to get into Westminster but have been offered a place there as a kind of top people's perk. As a result, male peers do not object to their women colleagues taking office; and the women themselves, having spent countless hours sitting on interminable committees with men, are not inhibited by any false modesty about their own abilities.

There is also another, more cruel explanation. The natural order of the House of Commons, whereby members clamour for office, is reversed in the House of Lords, where the Chief Whip has to beg and plead with people to accept some of the chores of state. The reason for this is that many members of the Lords are very old or otherwise quite unsuitable for office. Many of those who do not fall into these categories are far too interested in continuing their activities outside the Lords and hardly set foot in the place. So diligent, conscientious, intelligent women have far greater scope for their talents than in the Commons.

One such lady was Lady Stedman, whose initial misgivings when she entered the Lords at not being well-versed in Parliamentary procedure were quickly dispelled. She made her maiden speech on local government finance, and a few months later was told by the Chief Whip that she was being recommended as a Baroness-in-Waiting. She was doubtful, because she thought it would take up too much of her time. 'He said I would only have to come down to London for two or three days a week and I believed him; but I was conned. I said I'd talk it over with my husband, but he told me that he needed to know my decision by 10 o'clock that night! So I had to yank my husband out of a committee meeting he was attending to ask him if I should do it. He advised me to do it; at your age, he said, they won't ask you again.'

As it happened, Lady Stedman greatly enjoyed both the rather scattered duties of a Baroness-in-Waiting and the more arduous tasks of an Environment Minister. 'Nothing has been like the strain of fighting Hampstead,' she commented. 'I've mellowed a bit and have learned to pace myself better; I don't go at everything as if life depended on it.' She was also amused by the fact that at Environment she had to work with Anthony Crosland, John Silkin and Ernest Armstrong, all of whom she had antagonised in her previous capacity as a county councillor. She had had a blazing row with Mr Silkin, for example, over money for a school, and had written to Mr Crosland, after his warning that local government would have to cut back on its spending, telling him not to make silly comments about the party being over because in local government it had never begun.

Both Lady Wootton and Lady Serota had enjoyed careers and possessed convictions that might have led naturally to a desire to stand for Parliament, but neither of them ever wanted to do so, although both eventually held Government office. Lady Serota found her fulfillment in local government, and became deeply involved in the education service in London. She herself had been educated at L.C.C. schools and then at the London School of Economics, where she read economics, with local government as a special subject. The choice of the L.S.E. and the subject she read were both unusual for girls in the 1930s; it also turned out to be a fortuitous move from the point of view of her subsequent career. For she was at the L.S.E. under the aegis of Harold Laski, who advised her that she should never learn to type; this skill would inevitably lead her into a mundane job. Furthermore, Laski was instrumental in starting her career in the civil service, where there were very few women at that time. An assistant secretary at the Ministry of Fuel and Power happened to phone Laski to ask if he had any students who might come into the department, and Lady Serota was recommended. A career of public service then ensued, with membership of innumerable commissions and committees, until she was given a peerage in 1967.

She soon became a Baroness-in-Waiting, and in 1969 she was appointed a Minister of State at the Department of Health. A reference to this appointment in the *Diaries* of Richard Crossman, then Secretary of State for Health, provides an illuminating glimpse of attitudes towards women politicians at this time. Crossman needed a new Minister of State on the social security side of his department. '"Look," I said, "can I perhaps move David Ennals from Health?" "Yes," said Harold, "you can, and put somebody else into the Health side in his place. What about Shirley Williams?" I said, "Shirley Williams is much more C.D.S. [the Campaign for Democratic Socialism, regarded as dangerous to Wilson's position] than Roy Hattersley or Dick Taverne." "But she's a woman, it would suit you. Shirley Williams, that's a good idea." I don't know what to think.

'Friday February 21: I rang Harold again . . . and said: "Shirley won't do." "Yes," he said, "I agree with you. What about Bea Serota?" "She won't do for social security," I said, "she's in the Lords but she might do for Health." Yes, this was a possibility. Bea Serota, ex-chairman of the children's committee of the L.C.C., a very powerful woman, now one of the whips in the House of Lords.'

Lady Wootton, who was one of the first four women life peers, was always recognised as a woman of outstanding intellect; in 1967 she scored another notable first when she was made Deputy Speaker in the Lords. A former professor of social studies, authority on the penal system, economist and former governor of the B.B.C., she seems so committed to public life, and has such outstanding qualities, that it is perhaps surprising that she should never even have stood for Parliament. When I asked her about this, she thought this was the most interesting question of all about herself. 'I was frequently asked to stand as an M.P.,' she told me. 'Between twenty-five and twenty-eight years old, I worked in what was then the joint research and information department of the T.U.C. and Labour Party. One of our jobs in an election was to prepare notes for candidates to speak on and in the evenings we had to go out and listen to them. When I listened to what they were saying, I realised that I could never fight an election. I could never make such opportunistic use of the material as they were doing. I was asked to stand for Parliament probably between ten and twenty times, but I always said no, and found my own line as non-political Labour. I always did a job simply because I was interested in the thing.'

This principled commitment to the truth, and the recognition that there is little place for honesty in modern politics, was expressed to me by Lady Wootton alone among all the women to whom I spoke. Many others, including some who had been M.P.s, referred slightingly to the House of Commons; they said, for example, that it was easier to get things done in local government and that the Commons was a chamber of windbags, that M.P.s' behaviour was childish or unscrupulous or unpleasant in a number of other ways. But none of them seemed to recognise, or cared to admit, that the chief victim of Parliamentary politics is the truth and that the casual exploitation of facts for party political ends is one of the worst aspects of the system.

It is not surprising that it should have been Lady Wootton who took this solitary position, however, for her early life, as revealed in her autobiography *In a World I Never Made*, demonstrated that her character was as strong as her intellect. Born in 1897, the third child of classical scholars in a family where even the cat was named Plato, she had to do her lessons at home until she was thirteen years old – although her two brothers were sent to Winchester. Her nanny came to the family after serving the Keynes family, whose offspring Maynard was to become an even more distinguished economist than Lady Wootton.

Her mother was an intellectual woman of strong character who was never seen to wield a broom or duster; it was a bold step for her daughter to tell her that she didn't want to read classics at Girton but economics. 'Economics, I secretly thought, perhaps held the key to some of the injustices and miseries of the world by which I was greatly troubled,' she wrote. As a compromise, she attended first-year economics lectures while studying for the classics scholarship. She married, early and tragically: her husband, Jack Wootton, was posted to the front in the First World War two days after their wedding and was killed five weeks later. She fell ill before her finals, and her mother, she wrote, was worried that she might not get a first-class degree. Her doctor advised her that she should only sit the finals exams if they really meant a great deal to her, because it was medically inadvisable. So, out of a desire for revenge for the years of being exhibited as the clever daughter of the family, and for the lost years with Jack, she accepted his medical opinion and was awarded an aegrotat – a degree granted without examination on grounds of illness. The following year, however, she gained a starred first in economics, and two years after that she became director of studies in economics at Girton.

She met her second husband, George Wright, when she became director of extra mural studies at London University some years later. One of her elderly Conservative colleagues in the House of Lords said to me: 'Barbara Wootton is quite brilliant, you know, even though she's frightfully left-wing, but she's a bit odd. She married a taxi-driver, you know. Wasn't that an extraordinary thing to do!' But this was a false impression that had clearly passed into legend. George Wright's taxi-driving activities were only a temporary hiccup in a career that took him on to become a lecturer and an alderman on the London County Council.

Once in the Lords, Lady Wootton fought a number of significant battles to translate nominal into real equality for women peers. One such battle, which is still continuing, concerned the very term 'women peers', since they are often wrongly called peeresses instead. Peeresses are wives of peers; as 'peer' is a title for those who have been raised to the peerage in their own right, women who have achieved that distinction should be called peers as well. Soon after Lady Wootton arrived in the Lords, a lavatory sign was put up on which the term women peers was inscribed – but in inverted commas. After protests, the offending commas were removed within forty-eight hours.

Then there was the delicate question of the peeresses' lavatory. When Lady Wootton became a peer, her husband said he wanted to become the first male peeress and sit in the special gallery reserved for the spouses of peers. Consternation ensued when it was discovered that if he did this, he would have to use the peeresses' single lavatory – so the first male peeress was consigned, to his chagrin, to the front row of the Distinguished Strangers' Gallery instead.

Lady Wootton was among those who drew my attention to the curious paradox of the Lords – that women are treated more straightforwardly there than she has encountered anywhere else (and as someone who has played the role of statutory woman on innumerable committees she should know). Yet she has had to wage a number of small campaigns to ensure that they are not discriminated against in any way. 'There's absolute sex equality here, so much so that it's slightly tilted the other way. We've more places on the front bench [during the 1974-79 Labour Government] than nominally we're entitled to. But when we first came into the Lords, it was quite fascinating, because the four of us were asked if we would like a table in the dining room to ourselves. This only lasted for one day! One of the things I've struggled for in the dining room is that my guests should be served first, even if they are men. The waitresses just wouldn't accept this at first, but they've got used to the idea now.'

Lady Elles, now fully committed to a political career as a member of the European Parliament, has spent her life in voluntary service. Talking to her one snatches a glimpse of a way of life and set of standards which have now all but disappeared – even though Lady Elles is still only in her fifties. She was brought up in a household that virtually served as an extension to Middle Eastern politics as her father, Colonel Stewart Newcombe, was a passionate Arabist and had been with T.E. Lawrence in Arabia. As a young child, Lady Elles travelled around Egypt, Malta and Germany with her peripatetic father. 'In those days, though, one was kept in the nursery and so didn't see much of one's parents,' she told me. But when she was eleven the family returned to London, where they lived in some style. 'We weren't rich, but we had servants - three servants and a chauffeur. When he retired we lived in a very nice house in South Kensington with two living-in servants.' The house in London was always full of her father's friends from all over the world. 'Despite his convictions about preserving Palestine for the Arabs he spent an enormous amount of time between 1934 and 1939 helping Jewish families coming out of Europe; the house was always full of Jews from Germany. He was never antisemitic; there was nothing racialist about his support for the Arabs. It was for him just a matter of politics. I remember King Faisal who came to our house, and Saudi Arabian princes. And T.E. Lawrence was a very close friend; I admired him very much. He was a sensitive man with a wonderful sense of humour.'

She was educated at private schools in London, Paris and Florence before studying French and Italian at London University and going into the WAAF. 'At this time I was not political. I was never interested in politics, only in ideas and achieving things and doing things for one's country.' She qualified as a barrister, although she never practised. While her children were young, she wanted to stay at home with them, but when the youngest went to boarding school she joined the European Union of Women as a lawyer and did voluntary work for them, eventually becoming their chairman. She gradually got drawn into Conservative Party politics, producing documents on legal discrimination against women and comments on the Finer report on one-parent families. She became involved in such committee work initially through knowing prominent Conservative Party workers who were friends of her parents; her circle of acquaintances in the party then grew ever larger. Despite her interest in discrimination against women, she does not consider herself to be a feminist. 'I don't believe in feminism as practised by certain left-wing groups,' she said. 'I think it's counter-productive. But I thought there was great injustice towards women, which still exists, and I believe that women should play a role in society.'

She produced a pamphlet called 'The Housewife and the Common Market', and in the year before Britain joined the E.E.C. made about 700 speeches on the subject up and down the country. This, she thinks, must have been the main reason for her peerage. 'The Prime Minister's office rang up and asked if I was going to be in that evening. I thought I was being asked to dinner. When I got home, I found a letter on the hall floor asking if I would like to be a peer. For the first time in my life I was left speechless.' After that, she was sent as a Parliamentary delegate to a United Nations committee on human rights, and was made a special reporter on the human rights of aliens, as well as being appointed to the European Parliament in 1973.

She maintains that she has come into politics almost by accident. 'I never really thought about going into politics; it was only because of my specialist knowledge that I came in. I only find it rewarding in the hope that one can contribute in some way to changing or bettering a policy; I'm not in it out of any political ambition. Being in the House of Lords is very rewarding and I love it and I have a great opportunity to speak on matters of general interest that concern me.' She is disarmingly frank about the advantages offered to her by her own domestic circumstances. 'I took an interest and did my best for my country, but I couldn't have done what I do if I hadn't been a kept woman. I live at home with my husband and don't have to earn my way. If I'd had to earn my living I would have done something different; when I was young, I wanted to go into the Foreign Office. I've never earned a penny in my life. A woman with no financial means of support wouldn't have been able to do voluntary work in the way I did. Whatever I did, I took the line that I was going to enjoy it.'

Her husband is chairman of V.A.T. tribunals. 'He's outside politics, so this makes life simpler. He has his own work and interests so they don't clash. The only difficulty is that I've had to be abroad a lot, and he's had to fend for himself. What people never realise in politics is that you're still responsible for the laundry and asking people to dinner and going to visit your aunt in hospital. There are endless offices which fall to a woman, and if men have to do these things for the first time it's difficult. He is exceptional; he's learned to cook as a result, and he's done it extremely well.' Nevertheless, despite this evidence of the hardiness of her own family – and despite her own concern about discrimination against women – she has strong reservations about women with young families going into politics. 'I would find it hard to sit on a selection committee and choose a candidate who has a young family; I believe a woman should have the chance to look after her children at home. It's very hard on children to have their parents always going away.' But surely this conflicted with her own experience: she had, after all, been brought up by a nanny, and said she had hardly seen her parents in her earliest years? Lady Elles shot me a strange look. 'Oh, that was quite different,' she said emphatically. 'I always felt my parents were around. We were a very united family.'

Lady Phillips, widow of the former general secretary of the Labour Party, Morgan Phillips, suffered throughout her married life from the peculiar position of being in the thick of political activity and at the same time totally distant from it; being expected to act as a kind of surrogate Labour Party politician, and yet being treated as a piece of the furniture for the rest of the time. Since she became a peer, she has held Government office as a Baroness-in-Waiting, the first woman to hold the office; she also became the first woman to be made Lord Lieutenant of Greater London. But while she was married she was never regarded as a politician – or even a person – in her own right. 'Although I married a politician I am not necessarily a party political animal,' she told me. 'As the wife of a politician I was slightly inhibited, because they never divorced me from the General Secretary. I was constantly being asked,

even in ward meetings, what Transport House was doing. It was rather
like saying I'm a Catholic but I can't speak for the Pope. It became
obvious that I was never going to have a separate identity.

'I was irritated by being seen as Morgan's wife. It's a very humiliating
experience to be the wife of a public man. People would want to speak to
the great man and they would push you aside. It was also very
demanding, being the family of a public figure. People would be ruthless
and demand that you came here and there and make a great to-do. I
remember when someone asked for Morgan's autograph, the man said
to me that he'd better have mine as well because the nobodies of today
were the somebodies of tomorrow. The wives of company chairmen
suffer the same thing – you're not considered in conversation to have
anything to contribute. I used to suffer party conferences year after year
which I hated because someone was always being crucified. This may
contribute to the break-up of so many political marriages. The wives are
neglected if they live away from London, and if the wife does travel with
her husband she has to play the very delicate supporting role. Whenever
Morgan wanted me to go anywhere, I would; it was important to
support him. But he never saw me in any kind of inferior role; he was
one of the true supporters of women's lib. He wanted me to stand for
Parliament; he kept saying, have a go.'

There was no dearth of opportunity, had Lady Phillips wanted to
forge a parliamentary career for herself; in fact, she constantly had to
resist pressure upon her to stand for election. On one occasion she
almost found herself drafted as the candidate for Brighton Kemptown
by accident. In Brighton for a party conference, she was rushed to
hospital to have her appendix removed. While she was there, and still
not quite herself after the operation, representatives of the local party
came to see her and invited her to become their candidate. She made
some polite reply to get rid of them because she was not feeling at all
well, and to her amazement later received a letter from them saying how
delighted they were that she had agreed to stand. She had to pen a tactful
note to tell them they were mistaken.

Despite the fact that she had been made to feel no more than an
appendage to Morgan, she had managed to build up a certain reputation
for herself. In her almost desperate attempt to be recognised for her own
merits and not just as Morgan's wife, she became general secretary of the
National Association of Women's Clubs – and it was perhaps significant
that she was most concerned about the plight of isolated wives. 'I went

directly to the young wives in the new town estates because they are lonely and people don't appreciate that women are very isolated,' she said. 'I've seen such women blossom and become extremely capable.' She also did a lot of public speaking over the years; she acted as hostess at Labour Party summer schools and got to know a lot of people from local parties. But she still was not attracted to Parliament. 'I had a short exercise on the local authority in Fulham when I was very young, but really I'm not a committed person,' she said. 'I'm more of a doer; I like going out in the sticks and doing things, and really the Commons is a bit smothering.'

She herself came from a remarkable family. Her mother was a suffragette and both parents were early socialists, so there was a constant procession of Labour Party people to the family house in Fulham. It was her mother who first introduced her to Morgan, since he was the Labour agent for the locality and her mother was chairman of the party and Mayor of the borough. Lady Phillips describes her mother with great admiration. 'She was orphaned at eight and sent to London at sixteen as a companion to some wealthy woman; she had a fund of stories about the appalling way in which the poor were then treated. She described once how one person she was with used to buy rolls for breakfast and tear out the middle, which she gave to my mother and the other young maid, and ate the outside herself.'

Morgan died in 1963, and Lady Phillips was raised to the peerage the following year. 'When Harold [Wilson] asked me to come to do a job in the Lords he told me that I had done a marvellous job with the women. He gave me the peerage in recognition of the work I had done – but I'm sure it was in recognition of Morgan's work. I did feel it was an honour to take it on that basis. And I've been able to do lots of small things in the Lords. I try to go along on most sitting days, and I often speak in debates. I put women first because I think they have no powerful voice, which puts them at the end of the queue. Who will speak for the deserted wives and widows?'

If Lady Phillips was a devoted but frustrated political wife, Lady Elliot – who was one of the first four women peers – was entirely happy to consider herself, and be considered, the consort to her M.P. husband. Unlike Lady Phillips, she came from a background that was entirely steeped in national politics. She was born in 1903 into a family which she herself describes as having 'lots of famous people in it, peers and members of the House of Commons'. These assorted luminaries were related to each other by a tortuous family tree, since each of Lady Elliot's parents married twice. Her father, Sir Charles Tennant, was seventy-nine when she was born, and died three years later – but it was the family of his previous marriage which contained most of the 'famous people'. His daughter Margot married H.H. Asquith, the Liberal Prime Minister, and as a small child Lady Elliot used to go frequently to play with their son Anthony – later to become the film director – at 10 Downing Street.

'I was devoted to my half-sister Margot,' she told me, 'and I used to stay at Number 10 at weekends. Anthony Asquith was called Puffin – because he loved going on trains. I remember flying model aeroplanes in the back garden in Downing Street. I also remember seeing the suffragettes standing outside the front door, trying to get in, and Puffin and I threw our rocking-horse down on to them! I became enormously interested in politics from the age of eight or nine onwards. I had this tremendous political background; I remember Winston as a very young man, and going on the yacht *Enchantress* which was available for Cabinet Ministers. I knew Baldwin and Chamberlain and their wives very well. I was always passionate about politics, I really adored it. My mother was a staunch Tory but I was always a Liberal; in the 1910 elections I had a pram with a Liberal rosette on it.'

At school, she used to read newspapers she had taken in from home; this interest in current affairs distinguished her from the other children. She studied for a year at the London School of Economics along with people like Arnold Toynbee and William Beveridge. 'Father was very rich and left us lots of money so I never had to work; I've never earned any money,' she confided to me in the drawing room of her home in Lord North Street, a stone's throw from the Houses of Parliament, where she has lived since 1929. 'Our nanny was with us from the time she was fifteen until she was ninety. That was in the days when people had servants and houses and so on. That was quite something, what?'

Although she was a passionate Asquithian Liberal, she gradually switched her allegiance to the Conservatives. 'I worked for the Liberals between 1924 and 1929, after Asquith had been defeated. But I never cared about Lloyd George very much because I was a great supporter of Asquith. In 1931 when there was a coalition government I supported that because by then I was fed up with the Liberals; and anyway, it was no good being a Liberal unless you had proportional representation.' In 1934 her conversion to Conservatism was sealed when she married

Walter Elliot Elliot, who was then a leading Tory M.P. and Minister of Agriculture. The marriage was to become the most important factor in her life. 'When I married, I gave up everything else and devoted myself to his political life. I used to organise canvassing and groups of people and make speeches. I did an awful lot of speaking; golly, there was hardly a town in Scotland where I didn't make a speech. [Walter Elliot was M.P. for Kelvingrove and for the Scottish Universities.] If you're going to speak, it must be your natural method of expression. I can speak on almost any subject.

'I was asked to stand for Parliament myself several times but I never did while he was alive. Walter was a Cabinet Minister, and I thought it was silly to have a wife in the Commons and a husband in the Cabinet. I was asked as a Liberal in 1929, but that was a constituency where the sitting Tory member was one of my closest friends, so I couldn't do that; and anyway, standing for Parliament as a Liberal meant you were doomed to fail.

'I didn't mind being Walter's other half. He used to say I was much better at things than he was. He was a brilliant after-dinner speaker and brilliant in Parliament, and I was very good on the hustings. My husband wanted a partner, so I was lucky. He didn't just want someone to be the bottle washer. We used to talk for hours and he wanted to know what my opinion was and if I disagreed with him he wanted to know why. He wanted me to have as much say as anyone else. This was the undoing of Anthony and Beatrice Eden, of course. She just wasn't interested in politics. But Walter and I took part in lots of amusing things, like the Coronation and the Jubilee, and we were always entertained. When he became Secretary for Scotland we lived in Scotland and were always doing things together. Kelvingrove was a dreadful constituency; he only hung on by his eyelids. It was a frightful sweat. In the 1935 election there were three recounts. At the third count, I discovered that there was a whole box of 2,000 votes which had been overlooked completely! We got in by about 200 votes.'

It was hardly surprising, in view of her unstinting work in the constituency, that when her husband died in 1958 Lady Elliot was persuaded to stand in his place. Apart from her work for her husband, she had been a member of the County Council in Roxburghshire since 1946 and had moved up the ranks of the Conservative Party hierarchy to become chairman of its Women's Advisory Committee and of its National Union. She was defeated at Kelvingrove – ironically by a

MARGARET JACKSON, a former junior Minister at the Department of Education until she lost her seat in 1979. A metallurgist by trade she was determined not to be 'the sort of woman who has grey hair in a bun and wears lisle stockings'

ANN TAYLOR, Labour M.P. for Bolton West, speaking to journalists at a press conference in May 1975. When she was a sixth-former she enrolled at night school to study British government because her direct-grant school didn't teach politics or economic history

HELENE HAYMAN, Labour M.P. for Welwyn and Hatfield until she was defeated in the 1979 election. She has suffered more than most from patronising press treatment

SHIRLEY WILLIAMS as Secretary of State for Education attacking her Black Paper critics. One of the most popular modern politicians, she combines a sympathetic personality with a sharp instinct for tough politics

MARGARET THATCHER after her election to the Conservative Party leadership, December 1975

The window of a children's library in central Moscow displaying a poster of
Margaret Thatcher as a Cold-War witch, February 1976

woman, Mary McAllister – but soon found herself in the House of Lords. 'Harold Macmillan, who was a tremendous friend of mine, thought up the idea of reforming the House of Lords and introducing life peers and women,' was how she recalled the Life Peerages Act. She was more delighted at the peerage than she had been at the thought of becoming an M.P. 'Having been the wife of a Minister, it wasn't going to be much fun being a backbencher,' she said. She became the first woman to speak in the Lords and was then offered a Government post, but she declined. 'I had inherited through Walter a wonderful property in Scotland and was also chairman of an agricultural auction market, which had been his family business, and I would have had to give that up. It would have been fun to have been the first woman Minister in the Lords, but I could make a much bigger contribution outside. I started all the social work in Roxburghshire, for example. I was essentially interested in people and things; Walter was interested in the great events of the century.'

She has now left local government completely. 'I tend to go all out on something and when I've finished my contribution I say, that's it. They all begged me to stay on the council, but I would not. I found them my successor and then left them completely alone. Sometimes, they ring me up and ask me what to do and I say, I'm not telling you, I'm completely out of date. I hate people who say, it was always so much better in my day.'

Out of all these women, for whom the House of Lords provided their only route into Parliament, Lady Falkender attracted the most controversy – indeed, controversy raged throughout her career in Number 10 as Harold Wilson's political secretary, but it intensified when he made her a life peer. In view of all the fuss, I was surprised when she agreed to talk to me about her career, although by then much of the controversy had abated. Sir Harold was no longer leader of the Labour Party, and as a result Lady Falkender no longer attracted much publicity. Yet the extent of the fury that she inspired could be gauged by the fact that when one or two more favourable articles about her started to creep into the press, these were viewed in some quarters as an attempt to rehabilitate her public image.

The fury arose largely because of the influence she was said to have wielded over Harold Wilson during his years as Prime Minister, when he surrounded himself in Number 10 with an assortment of advisers, who became known as the 'kitchen cabinet'. Marcia Williams, as Lady

Falkender was then called, was portrayed as the most powerful member of this inner sanctum cabal, a kind of Svengali to Harold Wilson. Someone who assiduously put over this image was Joe Haines, himself an adviser inside Number 10, who launched a bitter attack on Lady Falkender in his book, *The Politics of Power*. In this book he boasts of the influence he thought he himself had over Harold Wilson's policies; his assessment of Lady Falkender is obviously heavily biased. Nevertheless, it is worth noting what he said about her since the same kind of allegations were also made by a number of other people.

Marcia Williams, he wrote, had a powerful and pervasive influence over the Prime Minister. People from outside were impressed by her charm and intelligence, but those on the inside went in dread of her unpredictable tempers. She concentrated Harold Wilson's ambition, marked out his targets and curbed his tendencies to ramble down the byways of political argument. She became, Mr Haines claimed, a substantial part of the burden that forced him to retire from the leadership. Time and effort were constantly wasted by the need to humour her, and cope with her sudden changes of mood and attitude towards people. She had a clear, incisive, sometimes inspired political mind, a determined, ruthless, magnetic personality and above all a total and unswerving loyalty to Harold Wilson. 'She met for a great many years a deep craving within him: for someone else to whom politics was meat and drink and the very air that was breathed; someone who, at her best, had a political mind capable of testing and matching his; someone who, again at her best, possessed a deadly ability to slash her way through the woolliness and verbiage of political argument to get to the heart of an issue. Someone who was prepared to devote all her time to Harold Wilson's service; and someone who, at the very worst moments, was always there.'

Remarkable, if true. The accuracy of his observations about the burden she became to Harold Wilson should be tested against the fact that Mr Haines is no longer in Sir Harold's employment – he left voluntarily, saying he had had enough – while Lady Falkender is still Sir Harold's political secretary. That aside, she was obviously in a position of considerable influence within Number 10 and, even by Mr Haines' account, possessed outstanding political abilities. So why did a person with her talents not become an M.P. herself? Why was she content to remain the general's aide-de-camp rather than trying to become the general? How did she react to the controversy that engulfed her? And what kind of family background produced her?

She came from a family which was somewhat dilatory in its political allegiances: her parents used to vote Liberal or Conservative, depending on how they felt at the time. The young Marcia developed her Labour allegiance, she told me, through her love of history, which she read at London University. She was particularly impressed by nineteenth-century social history; her interest in politics grew out of a developing awareness of social injustice, formed as a result of her studies. She decided that she wanted some kind of job associated with Parliament and concluded that this would mean working for an M.P. She never thought of becoming one herself. The first thing she had to do, she reckoned, was arm herself with secretarial skill, since she assumed that no potential employer would otherwise look twice at a history graduate.

So she signed on at a secretarial school in Hampstead with money borrowed from the local authority to pay for the fees – a loan she had to repay at the rate of 10s. per week which she was still paying back when she got to Number 10. She then got a job working as a secretary in Transport House, where she reckoned she received one of the best trainings for political work that could be obtained. She saw being introduced to the party at its headquarters as invaluable, since she thought that the Parliamentary party was only its outside arm and did not represent the real Labour movement. While she was there, she noticed that plots were afoot against Harold Wilson, then a rising young Labour star, and she wrote him anonymous notes warning him of what was going on. Apparently he had no knowledge of this fact when he appointed Marcia as his secretary in 1956.

'I never had any desire to be an M.P., although I loved being associated with it all,' Lady Falkender told me. 'I was in Parliament as a secretary with Betty Boothroyd and Jo Richardson, who were members' secretaries at the same time, but they wanted to be M.P.s themselves. The longer I worked for one, the more convinced I became that the last thing I wanted was to join them all. I don't like the atmosphere of the House; it's unruly, I loathe the shouting and the debates. Everyone works themselves up artificially, and in a sense that's not where the real work is done. I lived in a world that was halfway between social services and politics. I enjoyed the constituency business that is part of an M.P.'s work. I also enjoyed the backroom political stuff – the briefs, the propaganda work, what strategies to employ.'

Harold Wilson took over as leader of the party in 1963 on the death of

Hugh Gaitskell, but Lady Falkender maintains it was almost accidental that she eventually became an aide to the Prime Minister. 'Before Hugh Gaitskell was taken ill, I made arrangements to read for the Bar. I thought I would enjoy something different and that another training would be a good thing, and I had always been slightly drawn to the legal profession. I was about to start eating the dinners [a quaint ritual necessary for aspiring barristers] but Hugh was taken ill and died. In politics, it's never a question of what would you like to do next year; it's always in terms of a political event. So when he died, I thought I could postpone the Bar until after the first party conference, and then after the general election, and so on. It got pushed to one side. If I'd gone to the Bar, I might in time have gone out of politics altogether. If Harold had just been a member of the Cabinet or gone to the Treasury or become Leader of the House I might have gone slowly into legal work and disappeared altogether.'

When Harold Wilson became leader of the party, his secretary was confused about the role she was expected to play; and when he became Prime Minister, this confusion over her role provided ample ammunition for her enemies. The civil servants greatly resented her intrusion into Number 10; she was told, for example, that she would deal only with personal correspondence from local Labour parties and from constituents. She wanted to handle all correspondence from the parliamentary party, from Labour Party members and from trade unions. A compromise was reached by which she handled all the correspondence – but it was seen by the private office civil servants first. It was a classic battle with the civil servants, who saw in the Prime Minister's secretary an influence that might undermine their own.

There is no doubt that hers was a highly political influence, as Lady Falkender's own memoir, *Inside Number 10*, makes clear. In that book, she wrote from the standpoint of someone who was closely identified with Government policy. She spoke of 'our philosophy', 'our first day in office'; she commented, 'we had to fight a war on two fronts.' She was annoyed when the private office ensured that she was excluded from all the Prime Minister's functions during his tour of the United States in 1964. At Number 10, she wrote bitterly, the private secretaries hovered around the Prime Minister like vultures, often even accompanying him into the lavatory. 'It was an advantage they had on me since they could always give him their version of an incident before I could if he happened to pop in there before looking in on me in my office,' she wrote.

Now she attributes much of the controversy over her role to the theory that she effectively pioneered the post of political adviser to a politician, a role that was to become far more familiar in later years. 'I was always amazed at the great fuss made about me,' she told me. 'The critics implied that the influence I had was the sort that made Harold Wilson change his mind to do something I wanted him to do. That influence I didn't have. If you mean influence in the sense that I helped someone do something they wanted to do, then maybe I had that sort of influence. What they are really saying is that I was a buffer, and if you can't get through the buffer to the man they will always blame the buffer rather than the man. Most times when Harold Wilson didn't see someone or take his advice it was because he didn't want to; but to them it had to be that I was rejecting them personally. The civil servants thought I was a challenge to their authority because I was very political and they knew that he relied on the political advice he was getting. I was an obstacle in the way of complete control over him. They had had thirteen years of Conservative government and any political worker was integrated completely into the Number 10 machine. Conservative Central Office girls sat in the garden rooms [the Number 10 secretaries had offices overlooking the garden]; the civil servants had to work out a strategy for getting this new Prime Minister from a different party under control and I was a threat. I was even more of a threat because I was a woman, and they didn't quite know how to handle a woman being there. Harold Wilson happened to believe very strongly that a Prime Minister was head of a party as well as a Government and to do his job well needed to be political as well as governmental. If I'd been an old hag the attention wouldn't have been quite so fierce. But saying that I was a jumped-up typist was absurd; I ran election campaigns. I organised the office and I had to do the strategy side with him and take decisions for him, whether I liked it or not.

'The criticism was personalised and extremely wounding. If it had been just on the level of a woman in politics, I could have come to terms with it, but mixed up like it was it was very hard to take. It was a very powerful weapon to use against Harold Wilson.' When she received her peerage, there were some accusations in the press that Sir Harold had done it to spite the critics of his secretary who were, by extension, criticising him. Lady Falkender claimed to me that she had said this as a joke, but it had been reported as truth. 'More serious was the charge that it was like Caligula's horse,' she said. 'But people who have played supportive roles have been sent to the Lords before. People were hung up on their own prejudices.'

Whatever the motives behind her appointment had she made use of the fact that she was now officially part of the legislative machine? 'When I was given the peerage I intended to use it,' she said. 'But I came under such violent attacks in that last government that I couldn't move without being the subject of an attack and I got to the point where I didn't want to know any more. I take the view very strongly that until this is no longer the case I can't do otherwise. I've too much work to do anyway. If I knew that when I went to the Lords I would be able to operate free of all that, then I might have the desire to arrange my life to make it possible to go in. I'd love to do it. Over the years I've forced myself to go on doing things I don't like, but at this age I don't see why I should.'

I asked her why, in correspondence I had had with her, she had signed herself Marcia Williams instead of Falkender. 'Oh, nobody calls me Lady Falkender,' she said in a rather guarded manner. 'Everyone still calls me Mrs Williams.' Why had she chosen the name Falkender for her title then? It transpired that it was the wish of her aged mother because of its family connections. It was a touch of sentiment which sat oddly on this subtle, clever woman, yet her reluctance to use the title possibly betrayed her lingering embarrassment at being saddled with a name that might label her forever as 'Caligula's horse'.

7 Less Equal than Others

WINSTON Churchill told Nancy Astor, the first woman to take her seat in the House of Commons, that he found the intrusion of a woman into Parliament as embarrassing as if she had burst into his bathroom when he had nothing to defend himself with, not even a sponge. If one can extend Churchill's metaphor a little further, many male M.P.s have been squirting dirty water at their women colleagues in Parliament ever since that time, only receiving their come-uppance when an icy hose was turned full on them by Margaret Thatcher.

Most women M.P.s say that once the obstacle of the selection procedure has been overcome and once they have been elected for Parliament, the hostility and prejudice that they may then encounter in the House of Commons are minimal, and only take the form of trivial affronts. Some women insist that even this only exists in the minds of those who choose to see it. Nevertheless, one does not have to look very far to see the evidence of certain assumptions about the role of women in Government. With the exception of Mrs Thatcher, no woman has held any of the great offices of state. Mrs Thatcher became Prime Minister because she had been elected leader of her party, but the other three major Cabinet posts – Chancellor of the Exchequer, Home Secretary and Foreign Secretary – have never been filled by women.

Sir Harold Wilson, seen by many women M.P.s as the one Prime Minister who made a point of bringing women into Government, proferred me a pithy if individualistic explanation of the absence of women from these top jobs. 'The Home Office lives in the last century; the Treasury contains a load of mandarins; and the attitudes of the Foreign Office officials are moulded by the years they have spent among the Arabs,' he told me. Mrs Thatcher herself is known to have aspired to the Exchequer in earlier days, but to have concluded that no woman would ever be given the job. Shirley Williams would have liked to be Home Secretary, and was in fact a junior minister at the Home Office. But despite the fact that Mr Callaghan held Mrs Williams in high esteem, Labour Party sources say that he would have dismissed any idea of making her Home Secretary because he wouldn't have thought it a job for a woman. Certain other jobs are also male preserves: the Speaker of the House of Commons, for example, the Government law officers, and posts at the Ministry of Defence. Most women in Government – with a few exceptions – have filled roles which are thought suitable to their sex. They have administered health and social services, education, prices and consumer affairs. The assumption that women are only capable of dealing on a national scale with extensions of their domestic commitments to home and family still dogs them at Westminster.

The documented attitudes of some male political observers over the years reveal prejudices that have scarcely changed among some sections of the community. In 1929 in the *Manchester Guardian* Sir Alfred Hopkinson wrote, on his retirement from Parliament, where he had represented the English Universities: 'In spite of her brains, I cannot somehow ever imagine a woman Prime Minister. There is something lacking in her which a man leader has. It is perhaps what I should call mental tact. She is too interfering and unable to take things as they come without a lot of fuss, as a man will. If a man has to climb down and take second place – well, he just does so and does not mind, but a woman does not seem to be able to do this. It is this rather obstinate interference which I rather dread.'

On 24 March 1948 Mr W.J. Brown, M.P., wrote a double-edged article in the London *Evening Standard*, on the subject of the participation by women M.P.s in a debate on civil defence in war. Mr Brown expostulated: 'Into this debate erupted the voice of Woman. It is commonly supposed that women are the soft and sympathetic sex. The truth is that they are hard and unsympathetic. Their biological function, which keeps their feet very firmly on earth, and their minds concerned with eminently practical things, makes them so. That is why they are more deadly than the male. And no man is a match for any woman, whatever his armament.'

Leah Manning M.P. said during this debate that women couldn't be like men and contemplate fresh horrors so soon after the last war. Mr Brown went on: 'To describe the effect of this speech as "crushing" would be a triumph of under-statement. It was overwhelming. Woman had spoken and had swept aside with a dozen decisive thrusts of the housewife's broom all the litter of the male. We, the men, front benchers and back benchers, important and unimportant alike, recognised the note of feminine authority under which we had periodically cowered from our childhood up.'

He went on to say that he was all for making Mrs Manning Foreign Secretary – banter which hardly concealed the sheer dislike of women that poured through his article. Less blatantly hostile, but just as double-edged, was an aloof comment by Lord Altrincham which appeared in the *Guardian* on 29 December 1960: 'The right to vote, and the spectacle of a few women admitted on sufferance to a "club" still overwhelmingly male in character, are no substitute for the ancient and rightful influence of the political wife. The Braddocks, the Castles, the Summerskills and the Irene Wards are not to be despised; but they are like women who act as men in opera or pantomime. If wives lose their interest in politics, a mere handful of women politicians will not be enough to ensure that authentic female qualities are steadily applied to the arts of government and diplomacy.'

And if anyone should think that such attitudes have now disappeared, they should consider the opinions of Leo Abse M.P., revealed in his book, *Private Member*, which was published in 1973. His praise of Shirley Williams, for example, soon degenerates into generalised abuse: 'She is an engaging woman, outside the group of intelligent hysterics who make up an uncomfortable quota of women M.P.s. Her femininity belongs to her; it is not a facade, and because of this she does not dress in the vulgar exhibitionist manner of some of her colleagues. It is not their garish colour schemes or even their sometimes ridiculous attachment to clothes they could have suitably worn when they were young, some 20 or 30 years ago, which proclaim their difficulties; rather it is the droll display of nudity in low necklines and sleeveless dresses worn by women far too old, big, tall or fat for such caprices which is startling.'

After this splenetic outburst, he goes on to praise Mrs Williams for reconciling her private life with her professional aspirations. 'So often, prominent women active in public life, in and out of the House, are at odds with their own womanhood. They are continuously in a state of protest; and although their protests, often directed against real evils, result in needed changes, the shrill persistence of some women politicians, 'their ceaseless and humourless challenges and their exaggerated, impatient demands are absurdly disproportionate to the wrong they seek to command the House to remedy . . . I believe essentially many of our women politicians are aberrant women, doubtless not dissimilar from the women upon whose disorders Freud made his construct of femininity. They are endowed with high intelligence but are fated by constitution or upbringing never to attain a full creative femininity . . . Sometimes of course these difficulties express themselves overtly in homosexuality, and certainly there exists among women in public life more lesbianism than a naive community appreciates; but the only relevance to society of the masculine protest of women politicians is the distortion of some of their judgements on public affairs . . . The woman in the street recognises in fact that these political women are atypical members of the species.'

One wonders how our society would have reacted to a book that libelled some racial group in the way that Mr Abse libelled women. Such rubbish would be of no note – apart from as a macabre exhibit in some museum of anthropology – were it not for the fact that Mr Abse is a modern M.P., who moreover campaigns for restrictions to the abortion laws, an issue which is raised perennially in Parliament and with which the lives and interests of women are crucially intertwined.

Apart from expressing their overt dislike for women politicians – and even for women as a sex – several male politicians have assumed that women have a particular and distinctive role to play in Parliament. Indeed, this difference is seen as the justification for their being there at all: what would be the point, so their argument runs, of women becoming M.P.s if their contribution to politics was just the same as the men's? (At the same time, of course, women politicians are attacked for being different – hence the old chestnuts about their emotionalism, lack of logic and so forth.) The idea that women should become M.P.s simply because men and women are entitled to the same rights and duties as citizens doesn't seem to occur to these people. On 20 March 1936, for example, Robert Bernays M.P. wrote in the London *Evening Standard* about the Parliamentary debates on national defence: 'It has been for years a platform platitude that women, now that they have achieved political power on a complete equality with men, would be able to exercise an immense healing influence upon national and racial animosities. Yet in all these debates the women M.P.s have contributed nothing to our deliberations.' On the navy and air estimates, he said, one woman spoke on each of the two days devoted to these topics. 'Both of these speeches could equally well have been delivered by any competent male back-bencher,' snorted Mr Bernays in evident disgust. 'A few weeks ago, Mr Lansbury moved a motion on world peace. It was expressed in the most general terms, and would have given a splendid opportunity for a woman to propound a peace programme. I did not see a single woman even trying to catch the Speaker's eye. Yet at election time the major part of our propaganda is directed at the women electors.'

Not only were women M.P.s failing to save the world, it seemed; they were not even pleasant personalities. 'This determination of women to prove that they are just the same as men produces a certain harshness in their outlook. They take such pains not to be sentimental that they tend to resist the claims of sentiment . . . If they continue to take their standards from the men they will have as much chance of excelling over them in politics as a woman has of beating a man at tennis. If they [the leaders of the fight for women's suffrage] could have been present in the debates in the last few days and witnessed the wholly negative attitude of the women for whose freedom they fought, on the paramount questions of peace and national safety, I wonder whether they would have thought their stern sacrifice worthwhile.'

The former Conservative Prime Minister, Edward Heath, entertained similar views. On 16 January 1966 he told Kenneth Harris of the *Observer* that he would like to see more women in politics at all levels 'so long as they are providing what women can and not just duplicating what men can do – which probably would lead them to not making a women's contribution anyway. I've seen it so often: women on our advisory committees, for instance, coming up with ideas and approaches which apparently have never occurred to men, contributions which made you look at the whole thing again. And since politics becomes more and more about what concerns women, wives and mothers, you need their experience anyway.'

The women's apparent slothfulness on the great issues of the day was not only criticized by men. In 1950 the *News Chronicle* reported that Mrs Helena Normanton, who had become Britain's first woman King's Counsel, had said that women in Parliament had been a great disappointment. 'They come and they go; but what do they do? They go after the little-worth things but they will not concentrate on the great main issues. The great issue today is peace. Even equal pay is as a little mote of dust compared with the question as to whether civilisation is going to survive at all. We women earned the vote and won it but I do not think we have made the best use of it.'

Edith Summerskill, who was known – and often derided – as a militant feminist was, ironically, a contributor to the school of thought that led to women M.P.s being blamed for failing to make a unique and important contribution to British politics. For Lady Summerskill's feminism led her to think that women's contribution to society should be different, and better, than men's. She happily promoted the idea that women were suited to certain areas of interest in government. In 1953 the *Daily Herald* reported her as saying that the new ministries that were emerging at that time, which were concerned with everyday needs such as health, education, food, national insurance and housing, were near to the hearts of women. 'For women are constructive creatures who like making homes, and the building of a happy, natural home for our 50 millions calls for the same kind of interest . . . Now we have at the heart of Government ministries where the subjects under discussion are domestic ones. This is reflected in questions and debates in the House. For this reason, more and more women will be attracted to the world of politics and more and more people will recognise that they can make a valuable contribution in a sphere in which they find themselves very much "at home".'

This association of women with special fields of interest is misleading and dangerous. It is true that such domestic issues have been taken up by women; legislation on nursing homes, illegitimate children, adoption of children and battered wives – to list only a few topics – has been pushed through by women. But the issues affected by such legislation are by no means the province of women alone; subjects like health, pensions and education should equally be the interest of men. Their neglect in these fields created a void which women M.P.s found they were equipped to fill, but they then found themselves trapped in a stereotype which prevented them from moving into territory which the men in Parliament jealously regarded as their own. Lady Summerskill's notion that women brought special qualities to politics was rejected by every other woman in Parliament to whom I spoke. They agreed that because of the demands made upon them women often arrived in the Commons with a background of experience which men did not share, and that this might contribute to broader attitudes and a more down-to-earth approach, but that was the limit of the distinction they were prepared to make. The idea of special areas of interest was one from which they were all anxious to escape.

Yet women in political life have often displayed a curious ambivalence towards their position as M.P.s and their own desire for equality of opportunity. One of the most striking examples of this was furnished by Nancy Astor, who became a symbol of female emancipation by being the first woman to sit in the Commons. Less widely remembered, however, is how her Parliamentary career came to an end. She came into Parliament by succeeding her husband in Plymouth when he retired from the Commons to succeed his father in the House of Lords. In 1944, however, she retired because her husband had told her that *he* couldn't go through the stresses and strains of her fighting another election. An article in the *New York Times* on 2 December 1944 reported them as saying: 'Lady Astor and he have fought seven elections together and including the period when he was up for Plymouth have supported each other actively in the political arena for 35 years. It would be difficult for Lady Astor to stand again without his help.' The article went on to say that Lady Astor had told some of her friends that her retirement was a triumph for men. 'Today I have done a thing that has been terrible for me, one of the hardest things I have ever done in my life, but I think that every man in the world will approve of it. I have said I will not fight the next election because my husband does not want me to. I have had 25 years in the House of Commons and I am bound to obey. Is not that a triumph for men?'

This was a spectacular example of the reality of prejudice lurking behind the façade of emancipation. But this prejudice was not confined to men. In 1960 a controversy arose over remarks made by Lady Hylton-Foster, wife of the Speaker of the House of Commons, Sir Harry Hylton-Foster, and herself ennobled five years later. She told the *Sunday Express* that in her opinion women M.P.s were neither sufficiently educated nor sufficiently willing to find things out for themselves. Emrys Hughes M.P. raised her comments in the House as a possible breach of parliamentary privilege, and it was up to the Speaker to rule on whether his wife's remarks had constituted a contempt. He ruled that they had not. The *Guardian* reported on 13 April 1960 that the Commons was packed on this occasion. 'Mrs Barbara Castle had her Oxford head-of-the-river look, Mrs Judith Hart the cool and analytical air of the LSE, and Miss Herbison the combative alertness of Glasgow University, while Dr Summerskill – grimmest of all – stood for the heartlands of Kings College and Charing Cross hospital.'

There was nothing like the old sex war, concluded the paper's Parliamentary Correspondent, to bring the women into the House. Sex war or not, at least one woman M.P. was not averse to using her sex on occasion. In 1966 the *Daily Telegraph* reported that Barbara Castle, then Transport Minister, had taken the parliamentary press gallery into her confidence about the 'three feminine characteristics' which imbued her White Paper on transport policy. These turned out to be impatience arising from a desire to get practical results, her emphasis on transport policy reflecting social costs, and the importance she attached to road safety. Why these characteristics should be considered 'feminine', it is hard to see.

The contrast between those fighters for women's rights who believe that women should be regarded as a separate section of the community, and those who believe with equal passion that the best service that can be done for women is to treat them simply as people, was brought home to me by encounters I had with two venerable women, Lady Wootton and Lady Summerskill. When I asked Lady Wootton if I might interview her for this book, she declined at first on the grounds that it did women no good at all to be isolated as a special group. In a letter to me, she said: 'I'm afraid I take the view that the time has gone by when in professional or public life women should be treated as a special category. Originally this was necessary so that we could get the doors open to us; but now I think we shall find our rightful place in the world most effectively if we are accepted as M.P.s, or doctors, or engineers, or what have you, simply as people without reference to sex – which is important in private life, in marriage, and motherhood, but not in contexts in which we are engaged in exactly the same activities as the opposite sex.' (In fact, Lady Wootton did eventually agree to see me after I had replied to her letter pointing out that women were by no means treated as equals in politics, however much one might wish that this were the case.)

My experience with Lady Summerskill was quite different. I had wanted to speak to her at the very beginning of my researches, since I was aware of the scope of her experiences – she was then seventy-seven years old – and her considerable reputation as a feminist, which I thought might point me towards some useful avenues of enquiry. She invited me to call upon her at her home, where I duly presented myself at the appointed hour. It soon became clear that she had thought I was related to some individual known to her – which I was not. Upon discovering this, she inquired what had I done for the feminist movement. I replied that I felt that I had done nothing of any significance. She seemed much taken aback by this information. Well, what movements did I belong to, then? None at all, I replied. None at all? How old was I? And was I educated? Upon learning that I was twenty-seven and had been educated at Oxford, she drew herself up in her chair as if I had delivered some savage insult. Did I not know who she was? Did I not know that she had spent years of her life working so that girls like me could go to Oxford? Why in heaven's name had I not joined any feminist organisations while I was there? I replied that I had found them too dogmatic. Too dogmatic! she expostulated. Did I not know that she had such people visiting her every day, and they were all wonderful women? Just wait till they heard about this! And what was I writing this book for, anyway? Just out of interest, I replied feebly. Interest! she exclaimed. I was obviously writing it for the money. She had nothing in common with me; she would tell me nothing; and she thought I had better leave. Within ten minutes of meeting Lady Summerskill, I found myself on the other side of her front door.

I had cause to reflect on this unusual experience when reading some remarks of Shirley Williams which she had made to Dilys Rowe of the *Guardian* on 18 April 1960. In that interview, she said that she admired the views of her mother, Vera Brittain, without sharing them, and she went on: 'I'm not a feminist either, but that's a matter of generations, I think, don't you?' To Lady Summerskill, who has fought so passionately for women all her life, feminism must still mean joining up, identifying oneself with the cause, organising as a separate group and regarding all women as one identifiable body of people. Presumably the attitude of Lady Wootton, four years her senior, that women should be treated simply as people and not as oddities within a group, would be as intolerable to Lady Summerskill as was my presence.

The vast majority of the women whom I did manage to interview at some length did not regard themselves as feminists, although the majority said that they felt they had an additional responsibility to their task as constituency M.P.s. That responsibility was to women, whom they felt they should take care to represent since women were so grossly under-represented at Westminster. If there was a pattern of attitudes to be discerned, it was that the women who had entered Parliament within the last ten years felt this responsibility more keenly than those who had entered it thirty years ago, when they had been anxious to present themselves as equal to any man and correspondingly inclined to play down the fact that they were women.

The most outstanding example of this attitude was Barbara Castle. 'I always thought of myself as an M.P., not as a woman M.P.,' she told me. 'Being a woman here is something I'm not even conscious of. I never had any conscious determination not to take up women's issues – I have just not been particularly interested in them.' Yet she has pushed through reforms, such as the introduction of child benefit and the equal pay legislation, which profoundly affect women. 'Sex prejudice ran riot over child benefit,' she recalled. 'There were members of the Parliamentary Labour Party who said that they thought a man should do with his wages as he liked. We shamed them out of it. I didn't work for equal pay as a feminist issue; it was one of sheer, simple justice. It was outrageous that we should have sweated labour by anybody.'

A rather different perspective was provided by Jo Richardson, who became an M.P. in 1974. When she arrived in Parliament, she was particularly interested in defence, but she gradually became more and more committed to taking up issues which particularly affected women. 'On the whole, not enough is done about them,' she said. 'Of course, I represent all my constituents, but the more you open the Pandora's box, the more you find there is to do. The general attitude towards women seems to be – give them the Sex Discrimination Act and the Equal Pay Act and pensions and a bit of maternity leave and then say, you've got what you want so now leave us alone.' Abortion was an issue which brought most of the Labour women M.P.s together during the 1970s to try to prevent changes in the abortion law. One of the most pressing outstanding grievances is held to be discrimination against women in the tax and social security systems. Jo Richardson recalled a general attitude of 'here come the women again' when deputations of M.P.s tried to press for reforms in this area.

Both the Labour and Conservative Parties have women's sections, which hold their own annual conferences. Within the Labour Party, the existence of such a section is a point of considerable controversy, and I found the Labour women M.P.s divided in their opinions. Does a distinct women's section promote the cause of women in politics by drawing into the political arena women who might otherwise never become involved; or, by hiving the women off into their own section, does it perpetuate the impression that women are different and inferior, and effectively neutralise the contribution they might otherwise make to the party?

There are two arms to the women's organisation within the Labour Party. One is the National Labour Women's Advisory Committee, which contains representatives of more than 1,000 women's groups within the party. This body has a full-time officer, Joyce Gould, who is based at Transport House, and it holds an annual conference. In addition to the activities of this committee, there are also five women's seats on the party's National Executive Committee, which were originally created to ensure that at least some women got on to the N.E.C.

The existence of the women's committee and the women's conference underlines the fact that women M.P.s carry the burden of the 'second constituency' of women's interests. One of the most pointed and bitter attacks on this system, and on the attitudes that created it, was made by Lena Jeger, the widely respected M.P. who retired from Parliament at the 1979 election, in an article for the *Guardian* on 23 March 1964. She pointed out that conscientious political women were expected to attend not only the party's annual conference but its women's conference as well. 'Parties hold their separate women's conferences as if there were still any subjects under the sun that were the affair of only one sex. We all run our women's conferences as if only women cared about children, as if men were not parents; as if consumer protection was entirely the affair of tired little women with string bags; as if the soft-faced men who did well out of the war had nothing to do with costs and prices and profits and values; as if no man ever bought mutton labelled lamb, or cared about how his wife was looked after at the maternity hospital.' The separate conference, she went on, 'gives some condescending men a chance to declaim about how all politicians depend on the ladies who at any moment now will be expected to address the mountains of envelopes, make the tea, knock at the doors'.

Women M.P.s, she said, were expected to add issues like widows' pensions, maternity services and cheap milk to their Parliamentary concerns about world issues. 'Presumably you neglect southern Rhodesia, E.F.T.A., Algeria and unemployed school leavers to concentrate on the price of cabbages and the quality of nappies and then men will pat your shoulder and say that you are a "splendid little woman". For obvious reasons, many widows from all over the country used to write to me (and still do) to say: "You're not my M.P. but I'm writing to you because you are a woman and a widow yourself and therefore you will understand what I'm going through and why I can't manage on my pension . . ." I always want to redraft such letters, to readdress them to the M.P. for the constituency: "Dear Sir, I'm writing to you because you are a man and an M.P. and a husband and because you will never be a widow yourself and because you passed all those laws that crucify us with their earnings rules and their inadequacies and their meanness and because as a man you should be ashamed . . ." So we lumber ourselves with two conferences, two jobs, two loads of responsibility, without counting the home front and the job, which many women councillors and political workers run as well.'

The feeling behind this impassioned onslaught was shared by many of the Labour M.P.s to whom I talked. These women felt that a distinct women's organisation, and separate seats on the N.E.C., may have served a purpose years ago, but that in today's political and social climate such separatism does women more of a disservice. After all, what chance do women have of being taken seriously and treated simply on their own merits if they are organised as a separate group? If removing the five women's seats means that no women are elected to the N.E.C., Mrs Helene Hayman remarked to me, then so be it; at least then the party will be forced to face up to its own failings and prejudices. The idea of such an absurdity as a 'women's issue' can never be scotched while committees and conferences owe their very existence to it.

But powerful arguments were mounted against this point of view, not least by those women who had once shared it. Barbara Castle was for a long time vehemently opposed to the women's organisations. She was, after all, the first woman to be elected to one of the non-women's seats on the N.E.C. She had been elected to the women's section in 1950, but when she felt she was about to be eased out by the trade unions because she wasn't prepared to toe the orthodox line she audaciously switched to the constituency section and to her amazement was returned. But two or three years ago, she told me, she had changed her mind about the once despised women's conference which, like Lena Jeger, she had attended out of a sense of duty. She had gone down to address the conference, and what struck her forcibly, she said, was the number of young women who were making speeches which were highly political and about issues that were important; it was not the uninspiring occasion she had re-membered. 'On the train back, one of the delegates said to me how much she had enjoyed it because she could never get to ordinary party conferences, since her G.M.C. [party management committee] always sent a man. And I suddenly realised: I had always had a launching pad in a highly intellectualised and political background. You can't just say to any woman who hasn't been brought up in that kind of environment – go ahead and do it. That's a kind of élitism.'

It was the realisation that she had been guilty of a kind of blinkered arrogance in her attitude towards the women's organisations that turned Mrs Castle into their champion. She now believes that more money should be poured into the women's section – at present it receives less money than the smaller, and separate, Young Socialists – and that the women's conference should be able to elect at least half the women's seats on the N.E.C. Others have noticed the change in the nature of the issues discussed by the women's section, and that the women's conference has become a forum for ideas that belong to the left of the party and is no longer just an airing ground for women's issues.

But Renée Short, for example, feels that it is still important to push those women's issues within the party, and that without the women's section the voice of women would never be heard. The home policy subcommittee of the N.E.C. would have been highly unlikely to commission studies on subjects like women's employment or child care if the five women's seats on the N.E.C. didn't exist. The N.L.W.A.C. made sure that proposals for reforming the taxation system, improving low pay for women and nursery provision all figured in the draft election manifesto prepared by the N.E.C. in 1979; many of those proposals were eventually dropped, as were other N.E.C. policies, in the final draft prepared by Mr Callaghan, but that was not the point. Unless these issues were pointed out to the N.E.C., said Joyce Gould, its members wouldn't think of them, so a women's pressure group was necessary.

Among the Conservative M.P.s, there was virtually no opposition to their own women's organisation – possibly because it has always been acknowledged to be a powerful force within the party. This is because most of the grass roots work in the party's associations is done by women, and the most important work they do is raising money. Communication from these crucial workers is channelled through a hierarchy of women's branches and area committees to the party's Women's National Advisory Committee, whose chairman automatically becomes a vice-chairman of the party.

Lynda Chalker, a junior Health Minister in the Thatcher administration, was in no doubt that the Women's Advisory Committee exercised an influence over the party's policies. When the previous Conservative government had produced its Green Paper on tax credits, she said, it was the women's committee which mounted a successful lobby to establish the principle that the child credit should be paid to the mother in cash – the principle that later became enshrined in child benefit. 'Irene Ward [now Baroness Ward] used to almost batter Ted Heath with her handbag,' she recalled. 'She would tell him, he hadn't got a woman at home to tell him what to do, so he had better listen to her!'

However, I discovered dissatisfaction among some association workers with the W.N.A.C. Their main grievance was that in recent years it had, ironically, gained too much political influence; it had become an extremely professional organisation and as a result had become too remote from the grass roots. One woman complained that it was now dominated by intellectuals and high-flyers. 'In the past, the village postmistress could get up and say what she thought and it would have been the only forum for her to do this; now, she would be too intimidated,' she said. The women who were active in it now were younger than they had been previously; many more were university-educated and they were more politically motivated. Instead of simply acting as fund-raisers they now undertook surveys and questionnaires, and their influence had grown.

Personally, I don't think that separate women's sections within the parties serve much purpose – indeed, they probably do women a disservice. They perpetuate the idea that women are different within the political arena, rather like a minority group. Women are in fact the majority group within the community, but while they are regarded as special in some way they will continue to be seen as freaks in politics, whether they are viewed with exasperation or with affection. The women's sections, their annual conferences and the reserved seats on the Labour Party N.E.C. are anachronisms. Perhaps they were necessary at one time, but they are now an excuse to push women into a convenient slot. Among all the people to whom I spoke, none was able to convince me that these separate sections had played any crucial part in influencing policy. There were a number of issues on which they had been outspoken, it is true, and they had made a valuable contribution to the debate on child benefit, for example, or equal pay. But theirs were simply voices supporting the wider clamour for these measures to be passed. In terms of party politics, the separate platform of the women's conference or section possibly even provides the men at Westminster with an opportunity to push to one side what 'the women's lobby' is saying.

There are certainly persuasive arguments in favour of the women's conferences and the separate seats on the N.E.C. It is probably true that the women's conference provides a forum for women who otherwise would not be able to make themselves heard at party conferences or union meetings. It is undoubtedly true that if the women's seats were removed from the N.E.C. virtually no women would be elected to it. Powerful as these arguments may be, they are self-evidently not good enough. The women's conferences have failed to open up for women the route to Westminster; the women on the N.E.C. have not ensured that women are regarded within the Labour Party on an equal basis with men. The women's conference may provide a platform, but it remains a separate platform, one which simply enables women to shout from the sidelines of politics. While it exists, furthermore, there will be less impetus to improve women's representation in the main arena. As for the N.E.C., if the women's seats were to be removed and no women elected as a result, it would at least mean that the veils would be ripped away and it would no longer be so easy to ignore the party's fundamentally reactionary attitude towards women.

All the women M.P.s to whom I spoke, whatever they thought of their party's women's organisation, were keen to be seen as simply M.P.s, not as women M.P.s. One might therefore expect that, once they arrived at Westminster, they would be as keen to gain office as any man. But this did not appear to be the case. Among a sizeable number of them, I discovered a diffidence about their own abilities – which were often considerable, and caused them to be spoken of with great respect – and a corresponding reluctance to push themselves forward, to sully themselves in the indelicate business of self-advancement. Naturally, there must be men in the House of Commons who are equally diffident, just as there have been one or two women M.P.s who have been considered unrivalled experts in the art of opening the right doors for themselves. But such women are exceptional and the characteristic makes them stand out from their women colleagues. Among the men in the Commons, it is the diffident one who is noticeable. Lady Falkender, who as Harold Wilson's secretary for more than twenty years was able to observe closely the personalities in the Commons, agreed that this was the case. 'Men push themselves naturally; they are brought up at school to throw their weight around,' she told me. 'Men are not self-conscious in saying to the leader of their party how well their own records suit them for particular offices. I've seen it happen. It doesn't sound unnatural if you hear a man say it. They sell themselves more aggressively and better than women do; they know they have to. Margaret Thatcher is an obvious exception to this rule. Shirley Williams never pushed herself, but was surrounded by a group who were impressed by her and pushed her forward.'

Lady Davidson, who perhaps belongs to an older and more civilised political school, believes that she succeeded in politics simply by being nice to people. After she took over her husband's Hemel Hempstead constituency, she proved she was no slouch by becoming the first woman to be a member of the executive of the 1922 Committee, the organisation of Conservative Backbenchers. 'I can't remember any bad attitudes towards me,' she said, 'but it all depends on your attitude of mind. If you're nice to people, then they are nice to you. I did a great deal of speaking in the Commons and was on a lot of committees. I didn't want to hold office, however, because I didn't want to do anything that would separate me from my husband. We always slept in a double bed, and that's when I did all my talking to him.'

Renée Short was one of the women who told me that she had not been able to bring herself to push for a Government job – although she had been chairman of an all-party expenditure committee. 'I wanted to be a Minister,' she said, 'but I can't ingratiate myself with others; I'm only good at fighting for others, not for myself. The men suck up until it becomes absolutely nauseating.' But what was this mysterious alchemy which these men were able to employ, which turned hitherto un-remarkable characters into household names? 'It means offering yourself as a Parliamentary Private Secretary, complimenting Ministers after they've made speeches which may not have been all that good,' said Mrs Short in disgust. 'Most women wouldn't find that a dignified and desirable thing to do. You approach men here on an equal footing, and you are not inhibited, but you don't go in for that sort of thing.'

Janet Fookes, the Conservative Backbencher, was similarly hampered by her own delicacy. She has never held Government office, even though appreciation of her abilities has spread across the floor of the House of Commons to the former Labour leader, Harold Wilson, who told me he thought highly of her. 'There was a certain repugnance on my part to seek office,' Miss Fookes told me, 'and considerations other than ability have to weigh with the Prime Minister.' She did, however, chair an expenditure subcommittee for four years, and her discovery that she greatly enjoyed committee work, the nuts and bolts of Parliamentary administration, led her to nourish an amibition that one day she might become the first woman Speaker. Like so many other women, it was not that she was without ambition, but rather that, like Macbeth, she was without 'the necessary illness' that attends it.

Gwyneth Dunwoody, who was a junior Minister in the Board of Trade, and seemed to fall into office as uncalculatingly as she was drawn into Parliamentary politics, adopted a robust attitude towards M.P.s' ambitions. 'There are two diseases that attack people here,' she declared. 'One is the feeling that they are so brilliant that they must become Ministers and they become very disappointed if they don't. There's also the feeling that they have, that everything they say is wonderful. I'm basically lazy, but if someone suggests that I might not be able to do something or that I'm too stupid to do it, I go ahead and do it as well as anyone.'

She emphasised, however, that she had gained office by being in the right place at the right time. Luck, and the advantage of knowing the right people, seems to have played a large part in the careers of most of the women I spoke to who had held office, whether this occurred thirty years ago or more recently. Lady Bacon, for example, was made a junior Minister at the Home Office in the 1964 Labour Government. But before 1959, she had had no experience of home affairs at all. 'I was a great friend of Hugh Gaitskell, who was my next-door neighbour,' she told me. 'When Labour lost the election in 1959 he knew I was feeling miserable, so he invited me to help Patrick Gordon Walker shadow home affairs. I told him I knew nothing about it, but he knew it would take my mind off the defeat – and it worked, because I became engrossed.'

Even when Government or Opposition jobs were not the result of such neighbourly patronage, it still helped to know influential people. Margaret Jackson, for example, who became a Parliamentary Private Secretary to Judith Hart as soon as she became an M.P. in 1974, had been working for Mrs Hart already as her political adviser. Before that, she had worked in Transport House and had been a member of a liaison committee between the House of Commons and Labour Party head-quarters. 'I knew a lot of M.P.s, because I had been a key link-person,' she told me. A few months after the election, she became a junior Government whip, an appointment which she ascribes to the fact that the then Chief Whip, Walter Harrison, knew her from her work in

Transport House – and that he wanted to have a woman in the whips' office. From there, she went on to become a junior Education Minister; but before she took that job, the former metallurgist was becoming concerned that she was being typecast. Talking to me before the 1979 election, she said: 'I didn't want this job at all because I felt it was a woman's job. I've never had a woman's job but always worked on the economic or industrial side, and I'm frightened that if I'm away from it for too long I'll go the way of Judith Hart. I've decided that if we win the next election and I'm offered either education or social services I shall refuse because I don't want to become typecast.' We shall never know what would have happened in that event, for not only did Labour lose the election but Miss Jackson lost her seat.

Margaret Jackson felt that her Parliamentary progress was helped by the fact that she was a woman, which made her more noticeable in whatever she did. It was a point of view shared by Lady Pike, who a year after winning Melton Mowbray in 1956 was made a Parliamentary Private Secretary. Being a woman and winning that Suez by-election, she reckoned, made her noticeable; then the Prime Minister, Harold Macmillan, happened to want more women in his administration. 'I remember being summoned to Number 10,' Lady Pike recalled, 'and he was sitting at the Cabinet table, and spent some time giving me a glass of sherry. He was such a gentleman, such a clever man.' He offered her the job of Assistant Postmaster General, an offer that caused her some dismay since she was anxious not to give up her business commitments. 'He said to me, "I know what you're going to say, that you've got a business to run. When I first became a Minister, what do you think I talked to my brother about? The publishing company! And you can do the same." And of all the things I've done, helping to run the Post Office, one of the biggest businesses in the country, was one of the most stimulating.'

A different kind of luck also operates to help M.P.s with their careers. Lady White, for example, drew fifth place in the ballot for private members' Bills soon after she became an M.P. in 1950. This guaranteed her time to debate her Bill, but to her consternation she realised that she had no idea what cause she wanted to promote. 'I went to ask the whips if they had a nice little Bill on the shelf. The only thing they could suggest was a Bill about sheep dip and I felt that I wasn't going to throw away my important occasion on that.' Before long she was accosted by Marcus Lipton M.P., who suggested that she might like to put forward his proposals on divorce law reform. She thought the proposals, to liberalise the divorce law, were sensible, and cross-party support for the Bill was duly organised. In 1951, however, it became clear that a general election was in the offing. Herbert Morrison, the Home Secretary, was worried that the Bill might lose the Labour Party Catholic votes in marginal seats, so when he discovered the Bill was likely to be carried at Second Reading he was horrified. 'I told him that the Catholics were no problem, because they look after their own people, and that the real problem was the Mothers' Union,' Lady White recalled. 'But he wanted me to withdraw the Bill, and I said I would not. I was fully committed. So he said he would make certain it didn't go through. He found that we were going ahead with it; we carried the Second Reading on a very large majority, and he said he would still block it. He said we could either withdraw it, or he would offer us a Royal Commission, when he would say that it was a serious problem that should be examined from every angle. Eventually, I withdrew the Bill in committee because I couldn't see any point in going ahead if the Government wasn't going to accept it. The Royal Commission was set up, but it was very unsatisfactory because they didn't decide anything.'

After this controversial beginning, Lady White went on to become a Parliamentary Under-Secretary in the Colonial Office and a Minister of State for Foreign Affairs – one of the very few women ever to have held a post in the Foreign Office. She became an expert in the affairs of Africa and the Caribbean, her two interests; Harold Wilson thought highly of her. But then something happened to cast her out of favour. The Rhodesian crisis blew up, and Harold Wilson was attempting to reach a settlement with Ian Smith. Lady White, who concedes that she was never a party in-fighter, made a critical speech about his Rhodesia policy at the Labour Party Conference in 1966, which scuppered her chances of becoming a Cabinet Minister under him. 'Harold knew nothing about Rhodesia or the people,' she told me. 'He never understood the impossibility of adequate sanctions. I believed he was inadequately advised. But I couldn't prove he wasn't going to be able to reach a good settlement, and one had a duty not to rock the boat at that time. I think after that speech, he thought I was incapable of getting an impossible case across at conference. You've got to possess certain qualities when dealing with the temperamental side of politics. I always felt that after that Wilson thought of me, she's a bright girl, but . . .'

It was Lady White, who, as Eirene White, had attracted the attention and admiration of George Bernard Shaw when she stood for Parliament in 1945. He wrote to her: 'No Government can be representative or democratic in the absence and disenfranchisement of women . . . I know what I am talking about when I say that men can't be trusted to behave themselves properly in the absence of women where the interests of their better halves are concerned . . .' He went on to say that electing more women to Westminster was an urgent necessity, and that women with her qualifications and antecedents did not grow on gooseberry bushes. Five years later, he wrote again on the same subject: 'Many of the male parliamentary candidates in all the parties are mere party yes-men and superannuated gossips. Women, who all have to manage homes and rear and bring up children are practical, know where the shoe pinches and will vote for anything sensible and necessary, party or no party.'

If Shaw was one of the few men outside Parliament who believed that more women should govern the nation, then Harold Wilson – according to many women – was the only Prime Minister who actively and deliberately brought a number of women into Government. Lady Falkender, his secretary, waxed eloquent about this aspect of his time in office. 'Men are not very comfortable with intelligent women,' she remarked. 'It takes a very special sort of man to like their company. But Sir Harold has a very striking record of bringing women on. There's still a great deal of hostility towards women politicians among men in the House; the men themselves don't realise that they are hostile because they are dealing with a woman rather than with a man. Barbara Castle was a strong influence on Harold Wilson when she was his P.P.S. and convinced him then that women really could be very good. Many of these women were outstanding; at one point, Harold could have put more in the Cabinet. He would have liked to appoint people like Joyce Butler and Lena Jeger, who was superb, but he had to stop because he thought he had reached a point beyond which he would have been accused of overdoing it a bit.'

Curiously, however, when I saw Sir Harold he seemed anxious to play down any idea that he had deliberately encouraged women into Government. 'I never consciously brought women on; I just went for the best people,' he said. 'There were one or two things I was particularly keen on myself which I gave to be done by women M.P.s or Ministers. The main one was the Open University; I put Jennie Lee in charge of it and she made a tremendous success of it. And Barbara Castle's first job was Minister of Overseas Development, which was another of my new departments. These women were all absolutely first class, good party people. But if man A had been better than woman B, man A would have got the job.'

Men in the House of Commons who accept their women colleagues on their own terms and treat them absolutely as equals are relatively rare. Several women talked about the patronising attitudes they encountered in the House, the sexist abuse in the Chamber, the pinpricks of irritation caused by endless little sallies of offensive banter. Most of the women who claimed to detect this sort of thing were Labour M.P.s; most of the Conservative women thought that such attitudes were more likely to exist in the imaginations of the women who perceived them. But party prejudices played no part in the perceptions of these Labour women. They were particularly outraged by the way Mrs Thatcher was treated in the Chamber of the House of Commons – at least before she became Prime Minister. She was frequently subjected to offensive cat-calls; M.P.s would shout out 'Get your hair done', or call her a silly little woman; they nicknamed her 'Naggie' Thatcher. And, according to these women, the prime offenders in these displays would be the Labour Party men, frequently those who came from the north of England. Mrs Thatcher was not the only butt of these men's jokes; they would direct their attention at women from either party, with equally offensive results, if the unfortunate woman did something to draw attention to herself, however trivial that may have been.

Shirley Summerskill confessed that she was afraid to wear anything but the most unobtrusive of clothes for fear of the remarks that might otherwise follow. 'More people spoke to me when I got my hair cut than had spoken to me in ten years,' she said. 'Could you imagine doing that to a man? If you wear something out of the ordinary here, they comment on it. They only care about what you look like. We still have a novelty value, so whatever we do or say is noticed. A man can make a fool of himself and it will go unremarked because they do it all the time; a woman does it, and it becomes a topic of conversation.'

Women in the Chamber are often treated as if they were freaks. Helene Hayman recalled that, during a protracted struggle to increase the number of women on a select committee considering abortion legislation, six or seven women used to come into the Chamber to raise procedural objections. 'The men had obviously never seen six women sitting in a row in the chamber; they used to come over and say, jolly hockey sticks! or, who's the Madam! When I first went into the Chamber after I was elected and shook hands with the Speaker, Selwyn Lloyd, he said to me that all the Labour women last year sat at the back; and as he couldn't tell them apart because they all looked alike, I would have to sit nearer to him if I wanted to have a chance of being called to speak.'

Such attitudes extended beyond the immediate confines of the Chamber itself. Margaret Jackson was frequently annoyed and upset by assumptions that she was having affairs with various people in the Labour Party. Or people would assume that she was a secretary, a status which they assumed gave them the right to make passes at her. She was also put out by assumptions made about her career. Before she became an M.P., she worked for Fred Peart (now Lord Peart). 'He kept saying how marvellous I was. One day he said, "I can't think why you don't settle down and marry some nice young Labour M.P. It would be such a help to his career." I said it was very nice of him, but actually I would rather have the career myself. He looked totally thrown.'

The atmosphere of the Commons is still like that of a gentlemen's club, and several women said that this made them feel like intruders. They found it difficult to stroll into the smoking room, for example, unless they were invited in by a male colleague. They were also irritated by being regarded as convenient 'statutory women' on occasion, and being directed on to committees investigating subjects that were felt to be appropriate for them. Betty Boothroyd remembered being approached to sit on the committee considering a private member's Bill about the probation service. The M.P. sponsoring the Bill told her that 'he needed a woman on this Bill'. She refused. Jo Richardson, when she first became an M.P., wanted to go on to the defence subcommittee of the expenditure committee, but she was put on to the social services subcommittee instead. Eventually, after months of badgering, she managed to get on to another subcommittee dealing with nationalised industries. Renée Short was told, when she first became an M.P., that if she wanted to make her mark she should speak on subjects like prices and food. If women spoke on other things, she told me, eyebrows were raised.

Lady Falkender agreed that the superficial comradeship in the Commons concealed under-the-breath prejudices. 'It's more obvious when you're appointed to a job as a junior or Cabinet Minister; colleagues then tend to say things like, perhaps she's feeling a bit under the weather, or perhaps she'll dissolve into tears. They will draw attention to the woman's sex to get her policy halted. Certainly, women on occasion do use their sex, but they are forced to do it because if it is being used against them they have to retaliate. You can't go on pacifying and keeping the temperature down. They are slowly getting used to having intelligent women around them. They resent it; they integrate you, but they won't give you any acknowledgement. They won't attribute something successful to a woman as quickly as they would to a man. Men see that a very clever woman has that advantage over them, plus the intuition and the added dimension that women have, to understand on a different level, and they may feel that she has more advantages than she should have. It's slightly terrifying for them to see it all in one individual.'

In addition to these external pressures created by old-fashioned attitudes and male prejudices, women M.P.s have to cope with far greater domestic pressures, created by the tension between their public and their private lives. The life of an M.P. must throw a huge strain on the domestic life of either sex, if they are married and have families. The punishing hours that the House sits, the frequent interruptions to domestic routine created by the tyranny of the whips, the separation from home and family if they are based outside London – these all take their toll. A tiny number of women, mainly those who have no family or close commitments, allow themselves to be sucked into Parliamentary life until it immerses them completely. They like nothing better than to while away an evening in a House of Commons bar, gossiping about political friends and enemies. They surrender themselves completely to the claustrophobic magic of the place; all their friends and social life are drawn from it; they dread the recesses, and are impatient for the Parliamentary round to begin again. Many women, even those not as intimately bound up with Parliament as this, testified to the mysterious pull of political life. Those who had experienced losing their seats said that they had been desolated, bereft; they felt as if they had lost a part of their personalities. Most of the women to whom I spoke had lives and families outside politics. The tension caused by the pressures of the life, and their own deep involvement in it, which tugged against their domestic commitments, was very strong. And in addition to this tension, which must affect male M.P.s as well, the women had an extra burden: the responsibility of caring for their families, children or elderly relatives – which men in the Commons do not have to bear.

Many women M.P.s are either separated or divorced, as are many of their male colleagues. But they all said that the failure of their marriages could not be blamed on their Parliamentary careers. At most, they said, the pressures of Parliamentary life might have hastened the cracks in their relationships, but the foundations of these marriages had become rotten for quite different reasons.

Those whose marriages had survived all stressed how important it was for their husbands to be exceptional men, generous enough to put up with the frequent interruptions to their own routine, emancipated enough to accept that their wives led their own, demanding careers, interested enough in politics to be able to bridge the gulf between their lives and those of their wives. Peggy Fenner told me that she had married when she was eighteen a man who became 'the most marvellous husband'; the relationship had withstood all the buffeting it had encountered. 'He is an immensely talented man with a great life of his own and a great personality, and he is much loved in the constituency,' she said. 'He never knew when he married me what he was letting himself in for. If you are going to be a political lady, your husband has got to want it for you more than you want it for yourself. He has to be such a fan and such a support. You couldn't see him making a speech, but he is a very political animal, never gets bored by politics, and has a tremendous partnership with me. When I was a junior Minister I had to live in London, and he used to come up and have dinner with me, just to be with me; and I used to go home as often as I could.'

Sometimes the husbands of these women seemed to be even more interested in politics than their wives. Mrs Oppenheim says this was true of her husband, but he had always assumed that as the breadwinner of the family he couldn't have afforded to stand for Parliament himself. Ted Castle (later Lord Castle), Barbara Castle's husband, made what might be considered a supreme sacrifice for his wife. He told the *Evening Standard* on 13 December 1967: 'I always wanted to be an M.P., or else a barrister and an actor. But I decided in 1945 that Barbara's properties were greater; her contribution would be bigger. Then I was defeated in the Abingdon by-election of 1953. Some of my friends think it is tragic and to me it's disappointing, but I can truthfully say that I've never been jealous of Barbara's Parliamentary success. I live a vicarious Parliamentary life, and move in the circles I like to move in.'

Denis Thatcher, the present Prime Minister's husband, has always seemed more remote from politics, although he has always maintained that he doesn't mind his wife's fame and successful career. He told Kirsten Cubitt of *The Times*, somewhat poignantly, on 5 October 1970:

'I've always made it a practice, and this has worked tremendously well, that my business has to come first, for as you know there's no money in politics and we've got to eat. So when Margaret is late it's quite convenient for I can't always dash off home like the average married man has to if his wife isn't going to get angry. I've always regarded the fact that no-one is interested in me *per se* with equanimity. I've never grudged Margaret her triumphs, no, never in the slightest.'

Yet behind the façade of domestic equanimity, the successful woman politician may be suffering agonies of guilt over her fears that she is neglecting her husband. Lady White's husband developed a serious illness during her years in Government office. 'There had been a conflict of loyalties,' she conceded. 'There had been times when he had wished the situation to be otherwise.' Her removal from the Foreign Office to the Welsh Office turned out to be a considerable help, because she was able to delegate much of the work and was able to rely on a very good Parliamentary pair. 'When my husband became seriously ill, I wanted to resign my office but he said no, I was in an office where I could manage. I wanted to be with my husband all the time. I nursed him at home and just managed. He simply said, you must stick to the job, you'll need it when I'm gone. But there had certainly been times in the past when he had been carrying a heavy job as one of the biggest publishers in the world, and he would have liked a little more home comfort.'

Most of the domestic strain suffered by these women is on account of their children – although Joan Lestor adopted a typically robust attitude towards this aspect of her own life. Although a single woman, she adopted two children and fostered others – in the teeth of anxious advice that this might be misinterpreted and create a scandal. 'There are more difficulties, certainly, for women M.P.s if they've got children, but they are not insurmountable,' she said. 'Life is about hurdles and getting over them. Helene Hayman and Gwyneth Dunwoody did it; it's not the end of the world.'

But other women, including the two mentioned by Miss Lestor, were less sanguine. Mrs Dunwoody said that at one time she seemed to be forever travelling. 'For the first year here, when I had smallish children, I thought I would never not feel tired,' she told me. 'Every time I sat in a train, I fell asleep. With young children you've got to decide to be close to them.' Her former husband, Dr John Dunwoody, was also an M.P. 'We decided we would spend most of our salaries on rent, so we got a flat very close to Westminster. I had an arrangement with the whips whereby I went home at a reasonable hour and made sure the children had switched off the T.V., did their homework and went to bed. Then I would come back to the Commons.'

Helene Hayman found the whips less accommodating when she had her baby. A week after the baby was born, the Conservatives cancelled all pairing arrangements for several weeks, forcing Mrs Hayman to remain in the Commons while it was sitting. She wanted to feed the baby herself, so special arrangements had to be made to allow her to bring the baby and her husband Martin into the Lady Members' Room so that she could feed the baby in the House of Commons at all hours of the day and night. 'It was absolutely awful,' she recalled. 'It was the worst time in my life because I was so worried about the baby; I didn't know what harm I might be doing him by bringing him in at all hours, but I didn't want to stop feeding him.' And as if this wasn't bad enough, she ran up against at least one hostile reaction – from another woman M.P. 'Sally Oppenheim came into the Lady Members' Room on one occasion and saw us all there, including Martin, changing the baby. She said something like, "What on earth is this place turning into!" and went and complained to a policeman that strangers were in the room.'

I asked Mrs Oppenheim about her reaction to Mrs Hayman's baby. 'I thought it was all a very pseudo-business,' she told me. 'Helene Hayman and her husband together earn well into double figures and she had a full-time nanny. It upset all the women who work in the Commons because they all said they had had to manage with their babies on nothing like her salary. There's no such thing as having three-line whips day after day. There was no reason why she couldn't have fed the baby in the car and then come in, just like anyone going out at night. If you take the view that you want to be an M.P. and have a young family – I'm not saying it's wrong, but I personally couldn't have done it – then you have to do it on the terms that exist.'

Other women found that coping with their families was a great strain. Shirley Williams, after her marriage broke up in the early 1970s, found she was having to juggle her responsibilities as a Minister with those of a single parent. While she was Secretary of State for Education, she told me: 'I certainly find I'm pushed to the limit of impossibility. You get your sleep down to $5\frac{1}{2}$ hours a night. The basic question is how you fit everything in; it all comes back to you. After I get home with my red box I have to make the dinner and by the time I start on my box it's half past eleven at night. I manage it because I am physically terribly strong, and I live nearby and I dash to and fro. And I used to have a good daily help. But there's very little time for private or domestic life.'

When Judith Hart became an M.P., she left her husband, a university lecturer, and her children in Scotland and tried to live away from them in London; but the experimental parting soon had to stop. When she returned home at weekends she found she couldn't tolerate having missed out on all the family's experiences during the week. 'For the children, just the knowledge that you weren't sleeping in the same house at nights and never being able to see you in the mornings and evenings wasn't fair to them,' she said. So her husband found a job in the London area and the family moved down, complete with Dame Judith's mother-in-law who lived with them. Even then, she said, domestic arrangements were far from easy. 'My mother-in-law was getting older, we were living in a house that was too small to accommodate an au pair, and one was continually having to juggle with domestic help.'

Ann Taylor, however, who was a junior whip in the last Labour administration, decided when she became an M.P. that she and her husband would have to put up with weekly separations, since he is a bridge engineer and would find it difficult to get a job in London. Furthermore, when she was first elected in 1974 she had a majority of less than 1,000, and with a tiny Government majority in the Commons she decided that the process of uprooting her family home might not be completed until the next election – when she could well lose her seat. 'With hindsight, we would have moved here. Of course, it's difficult; it's a peculiar life. It helps that my husband is politically interested, and that his family live in Bolton near him. I did think of having children during the last Parliament, but I never quite managed to work out the geography of it all.'

Barbara Castle has speculated that if she had had children, her political career might have taken a quite different course. Janet Fookes, who has remained unmarried, told me that her overriding interest in politics certainly contributed to the fact that she never married. 'One or two men were eligible, but they weren't quite right,' she told me. 'One said he wouldn't want me to have the limelight, and the other said he wasn't prepared to become a baby-sitter. I would like to have been married, but didn't meet anyone with whom it all gelled; and I would have wanted both lives.'

The sacrifices made by all these women M.P.s, and by their families, are by no means negligible. Women with families carry the double

burden of their Parliamentary careers and their domestic responsibilities; and with that double burden goes the guilt or unease that they are
not paying sufficient attention to people who need them. That burden,
with its associated anxieties, has not diminished over the years, but
rather has increased. Women M.P.s should, however, accept a third type
of burden – one which their pioneering predecessors accepted but which
is less in evidence today. This is the responsibility they have towards
women in the community. The cause of women presents an unavoidable
dilemma. There should not be such things as 'women's subjects'; but if
certain issues which affect women in their daily lives are consistently
ignored by men, women have no alternative but to agitate for these
issues to be reformed, thus creating and perpetuating the 'women's
subjects'. There is no doubt that issues arising from family life, such as
health, education or child-rearing, should be of as much concern to men
as they are to women; there is equally no doubt that they are not. This
arises from traditional assumptions that it is the job of women to take
care of these issues in their domestic lives. Until this illogical and unfair
division of responsibility is broken down in the home, sex equality will
remain a distant and unlikely goal. Women's subjects, including sex
discrimination, should not be classified as such, least of all by women
themselves. Nevertheless, unless women lobby on their own behalf, and
on behalf of their children, these issues will never be taken up. This is a
fact of life that is not peculiar to women but to any aggrieved group
which perceives that its best interests are not being served.

There are at present many injustices which women M.P.s should be
taking up; the relatively high number of stillbirths and deaths among
new-born infants, the lack of adequate child-care for working mothers,
continued inequality in rates of pay, and discrimination within the tax
system are all issues which, if not taken up by women, stand little chance
of being taken up at all. It might be thought that there is some conflict
between urging women M.P.s to take up issues like these, and urging the
political parties to do away with their separate women's structures. This
is not the case. Separate structures hive off women and their problems.
The cause of women is better served in the main political forum, where
women participate on an equal basis with men. Both men and women
M.P.s should, ideally, view 'women's issues' as items of simple justice
which are necessary to make our society a better place in which to live.
This, unfortunately, is unlikely to be the case, and it is up to women to
press for these reforms. They should, therefore, do this, mindful of the

women who helped elect them to Parliament. To use an analogy, if there were nineteen black M.P.s one would expect them to put the case for their communities, to speak out against racial discrimination and so on – but one would not expect the political parties to contain separate black sections and hold black members' conferences. Some women do accept this responsibility, but by no means all. Most are afraid that if they do so they will be perceived to be simply 'women M.P.s' rather than politicians. It is a delicate line they must tread if they want to strengthen the case of women in Parliament as well as fight for women in the community.

But why do these women undertake any of the burdens of Parliamentary life? What is the compulsion that drives them on to brave insults, intrusions into their private lives and domestic upheavals? Many of them are fundamentally reserved, diffident women, unwilling to push themselves into Parliamentary office that will bring them national fame. The majority were not possessed at an early age by a desperate desire to become an M.P. It seems, though, that once drawn into politics most of them soon fell prey to its curious magnetism: the compulsive, snowballing attraction of political life. From the humblest Backbencher who may never even have put forward a private member's Bill, to the Prime Minister who has the power to save or destroy the country, they all seem to suffer the same affliction. One is tempted, however, to give the last word to Denis Thatcher, who qualified his previous enthusiasm for his wife's career in this way: 'Well, we all get depressed and tired sometimes, don't we? I mean, sometimes one does sit down and think, Jesus wept – excuse my language – is it all worthwhile?'

Select Bibliography and Further Reading

Abse, Leo; *Private Member*, Macdonald, 1973

Atholl, Katherine, Duchess of; *Working Partnership*, Arthur Barker, 1958

Brittain, Vera; *Lady Into Woman*, Dakers, 1953

Brookes, Pamela; *Women at Westminster*, Peter Davies, 1967

Cosgrave, Patrick; *Margaret Thatcher: A Tory and her Party*, Hutchinson, 1978

Crossman, R.H.S.; *The Diaries of a Cabinet Minister*, Hamish Hamilton and Jonathan Cape, 1975–77

Currell, Melville; *Political Woman*, Croom Helm, 1974

Gardiner, George; *Margaret Thatcher*, William Kimber, 1975

Haines, Joe; *The Politics of Power*, Jonathan Cape, 1977

Hollis, Patricia; *Women in Public: The Women's Movement 1850–1900*, George Allen and Unwin, 1979

Lewis, Russell; *Margaret Thatcher*, Routledge and Kegan Paul, 1975

Mann, Jean; *Woman in Parliament*, Odhams, 1962

Margach, James; *The Abuse of Power*, W.H. Allen, 1978

Middleton, Lucy (ed.); *Women in the Labour Movement*, Croom Helm, 1977

Money, Ernle; *Margaret Thatcher*, Frewin, 1976

Stobaugh, Beverley Parker; *Women and Parliament*, Exposition University, 1978

Summerskill, Edith; *A Woman's World*, Heinemann, 1967

Vallance, Elizabeth; *Women in the House*, Athlone press, 1979

Wilkinson, Ellen; *Peeps at Politicians*, Philip Allan and Co, 1930

Williams, Marcia; *Inside Number 10*, Weidenfeld and Nicholson, 1972

Wootton, Barbara; *In a World I Never Made*, George Allen and Unwin, 1967

Index